DESIGN AND ANALYSIS OF ALGORITHMS

DESIGN AND ANALYSIS OF ALGORITHMS

By

SHWETA BAJAJ MUNDRA

Assistant Professor, MCA

Medicaps Institute of Technology & Management,
Indore (MP)

UNIVERSITY SCIENCE PRESS

(An Imprint of Laxmi Publications Pvt. Ltd.)

BANGALORE • CHENNAI • COCHIN • GUWAHATI • HYDERABAD
JALANDHAR • KOLKATA • LUCKNOW • MUMBAI • RANCHI
NEW DELHI • BOSTON, USA

Published by

UNIVERSITY SCIENCE PRESS

(An Imprint of Laxmi Publications Pvt. Ltd.)

113, Golden House, Darya Ganj,
New Delhi-110 002

Phone : 011-43 53 25 00
Fax : 011-43 53 25 28

www.laxmipublications.com
info@laxmipublications.com

First Edition : 2013

OFFICES

✆ **Bangalore**	080-26 75 69 30	✆ **Jalandhar**	0181-222 12 72
✆ **Chennai**	044-24 34 47 26	✆ **Kolkata**	033-22 27 43 84
✆ **Cochin**	0484-237 70 04, 405 13 03	✆ **Lucknow**	0522-220 99 16
✆ **Guwahati**	0361-254 36 69, 251 38 81	✆ **Mumbai**	022-24 91 54 15, 24 92 78 69
✆ **Hyderabad**	040-24 65 23 33	✆ **Ranchi**	0651-220 44 64

UDA-9678-125-DESIGN ANA ALGORITHM-MUN C—

Typeset at : Goswami Associates, Delhi. Printed at: Repro Knowledgecast Limited, Thane

FOREWORD

Mastering Computer Algorithm is not only essential but also is the requirement for any computer expert. Without having expertise in development of any program one can not be called a true "Computer Master".

A Computer Science & Engineering student always strives towards his long journey through first step of mastering algorithm. To develop a computer application, student must start from various phases of algorithm, *viz.* the Nature, Design, Techniques, Development, Testing and Analysis of algorithm. This book encompasses every aspect of algorithm such as properties of algorithm, expressing and classification of algorithm, life cycle of algorithm, types of analysis and specification of algorithm.

The book has been written in a very simple language which helps the student to grasp the content easily. It covers all the facets of algorithm with suitable examples which all lacking in most of the contemporary text available. A chapter on Data Structure is also included as it is pre-requisite for the development of algorithm.

I wish that the effort of Ms Shweta Bajaj Mundra will be fruitful and the student will gain knowledge of the subject with ease and expertise.

Sunil K. Somani
Director, Medicaps Institute of Technology & Management, Indore

PREFACE

"As we enjoy great advantages from the inventions of others, we should be glad of an opportunity to serve others by any Invention of ours, and this we should do freely and generously."

—Benjamin Franklin, quoted in *Benjamin Franklin* by Edmund S. Morgan

I started writing this book in September 2009, when I was teaching in first lecture of introduction on **"Analysis and Design of Algorithms"**. Student asked me—"Madam which book should we prefer?" I was answerless, because the books available in the market on this topic are too big! There was no way my students would read 700 pages of dense, technical material in a semester with other four technical theoretical subjects. All those books had very tough vocabulary which is not easily understandable.

The contents of this book are based on syllabuses of BE, MCA, MCM, M.Sc. (CS), and M.Tech. courses offered by various technical universities.

This book is written in such a way that it would satisfy requirement of future technocrats. An introductory chapter (Chapter 1) covers all the aspects of algorithm. There are solved numericals on the topics like Matrix Chain Multiplication, Longest Common Subsequence, Traveling Salesman Problem, and knapsack problem, to help you master the concept of algorithm.

—Author

ACKNOWLEDGEMENTS

Writing a book is similar to entering a long-term relationship with an obsessive partner. This job demanded constant attention. Therefore, I'd like to thank the people that made it possible to focus on the book to the exclusion of nearly everything else. My husband (Madhusudan Mundra, Quality Assurance Executive, Ranbaxy, Dewas), my parents (Especially my mummy who always dreamt for me to reach at apogee), my in-laws and my brother, Anand Bajaj supported and encouraged me throughout the execution of this project. Additionally, my husband acted as my editor and indexer, eventually reading the book completely three times!

Thanks also to my students, Medicaps Institute 2010 passout batch who inspire me to write this book. Thanks to my CEO Dr Shamsher Singh, Director Dr Sunil Kumar Somani, Dr Brijmohan Singhi and my HOD Mr Anil Patidar without whom boundless patience, my many questions would have gone unanswered, and this book would have been much less than it is now. I hope you find this book a worthy companion to enhance your knowledge.

Thanks to Medicaps Institute and Laxmi Publications Pvt. Ltd., New Delhi which help me to provide a platform to share my knowledge with the students.

—Author

CONTENTS

Chapter 1 INTRODUCTION TO ALGORITHM

1.1 INTRODUCTION

'A finite set of unambiguous instructions performed in a prescribed sequence to achieve a goal'

-Anonymous

The etymology of the word Algorithm dates back to the 8th Century A.D. The word **Algorithm** is derived from the name of the Persian author **"Abu Jafar Mohammad ibn Musa al Khowarizmi".** He was a great mathematician who was born around 780 AD in Baghdad. He worked on, algebra, geometry, and astronomy.

An algorithm is the step-by-step solution to a certain problem. The problem need not be technical, or related to computer. There are several definitions for the notation of an algorithm. As an introduction to the concept, we shall study some simple applications. like, In mathematics, computing, linguistics, and related subjects, an algorithm is a finite sequence of instructions, an explicit, step-by-step procedure for solving a problem, often used for calculation and data processing. It is formally a type of effective method in which a list of well-defined instructions for completing a task, will when given an initial state, proceed through a well-defined series of successive states, eventually terminating in an end-state. The transition from one state to the next is not necessarily deterministic; some algorithms, known as probabilistic algorithms, incorporate randomness.

1.2 PROPERTIES OF ALGORITHM

An algorithm has five properties as follows:

(*a*) ***Finiteness:*** An algorithm should end in a finite number of steps.

(*b*) ***Definiteness:*** Every step of an algorithm should be clear and unambiguously defined.

(*c*) ***Input:*** The input of an algorithm can either be given interactively by the user or generated internally.

(*d*) ***Output:*** An algorithm should have at least one output.

(*e*) ***Effectiveness:*** Every step in the algorithm should be easy to understand and prove using paper and pencil.

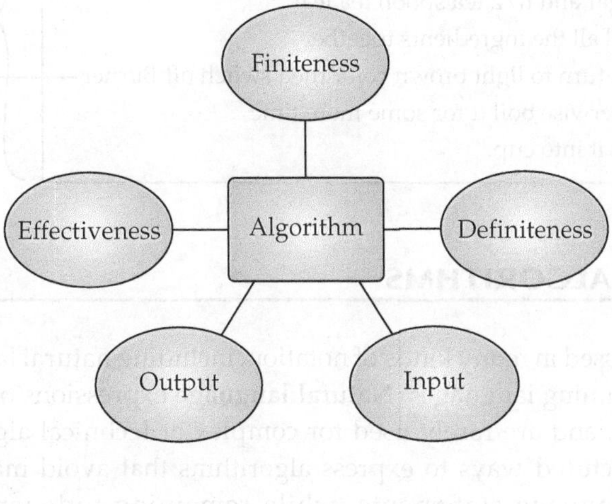

Fig. 1.1. Properties of Algorithm

1.3 EXAMPLES OF ALGORITHMS

(*a*) Recipe Book.

(*b*) Traveling plan.

(*c*) Designing Process of hardware or software.

Now, the given three activities above might seem easy but as you are to perform the task, a series of trial-and-error activities that you will encounter will be numerous, suppose you are going to prepare a cup of tea for that you have to follow some steps like:

(*a*) Get a Pot.

(*b*) On the Burner.

(*c*) Take ½ cup milk, ½ cup water, 1 tea spoon sugar and ½ tea spoon tea leaf.

(*d*) Boil all the ingredients together.

(*e*) If it turn to light brown color then switch off Burner.

(*f*) Otherwise boil it for some more time.

(*g*) Put it into cup.

If we have to prepare cup of tea for **"n"** person then ingredients and condition will change like this:

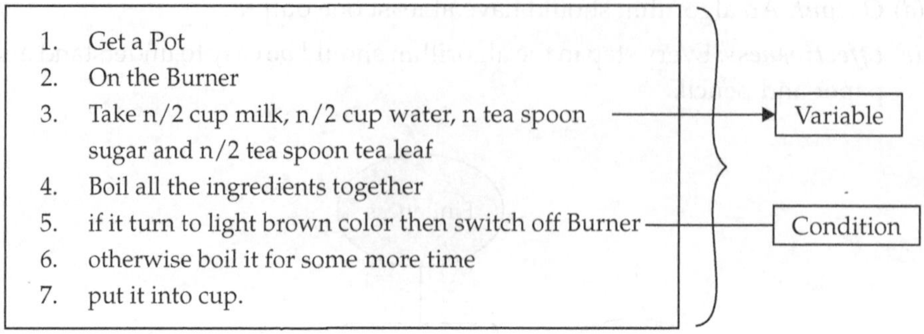

1.4 EXPRESSING ALGORITHMS

Algorithms can be expressed in many kinds of notation, including natural languages, pseudo code, flowcharts, and programming languages. **Natural language** expressions of algorithms tend to be verbose and ambiguous, and are rarely used for complex or technical algorithms. **Pseudo code** and **flowcharts** are structured ways to express algorithms that avoid many of the ambiguities common in natural language statements, while remaining independent of a particular implementation language. **Programming languages** are primarily intended for expressing algorithms in a form that can be executed by a computer:

(*a*) ***High-level description:*** This is a process to describe an algorithm, ignoring the implementation details. At this level we do not need to mention how the machine manages its tape or head.

(*b*) ***Implementation description:*** This is a process used to define the way the Turing machine uses its head and the way that it stores data on its tape. At this level we do not give details of states or transition function.

(*c*) ***Formal description:*** Most detailed, lowest level, gives the Turing machine's "state table".

1.5 CLASSIFICATION OF ALGORITHM

A computer program is another pervasive example of an algorithm. Every computer program is simply a series of instructions in a specific order, designed to perform a specific task. Most conceptions of the human brain define all behavior—from the acquisition of food to falling in love—as the result of a complex algorithm, while there is no universally accepted breakdown for the various types of algorithms, there are common classes that algorithms are frequently agreed to belong to. Few among these are:

(*a*) ***Dynamic Programming Algorithms:*** This class remembers older results and attempts to use this to speed the process of finding new results.

(*b*) ***Greedy Algorithms:*** Greedy algorithms attempt not only to find a solution, but to find the ideal solution to any given problem.

(*c*) ***Brute Force Algorithms:*** The brute force approach starts at some random point and iterates through every possibility until it finds the solution.

(*d*) ***Randomized Algorithms:*** This class includes any algorithm that uses a random number at any point during its process.

(*e*) ***Branch and Bound Algorithms:*** Branch and bound algorithms form a tree of sub-problemsto the primary problem, following each branch until it is either solved or lumped in with another branch.

(*f*) ***Simple Recursive Algorithms:*** This type of algorithm goes for a direct solution immediately, then backtracks to find a simpler solution.

(*g*) ***Backtracking Algorithms:*** Backtracking algorithms test for a solution, if one is found the algorithm has solved, if not it recurs once and tests again, continuing until a solution is found.

(*h*) ***Divide and Conquer Algorithms:*** A divide and conquer algorithm is similar to a branch and bound algorithm, except it uses the backtracking method of recurring in tandem with dividinga problem into sub-problems.

In addition to these general classes, algorithms may also be divided into two primary groups: **serial algorithms**, which are designed for serial execution, wherein each operation is enacted in a linear order; and **parallel algorithms**, used with computers running parallel processors (as well as existing in the natural world in the case of, for example, genetic mutation over a species), wherein a number of operations are run in parallel.

1.6 LIFE CYCLE OF ALGORITHM

The life cycle of an algorithm consists of the four phases:

(*a*) Design (*b*) Write (Implementation)

(*c*) Test (*d*) Analyze

(*a*) ***Design:*** Design is first phase of an algorithm life cycle. By using some predefine techniques we generally design our algorithm. The design techniques help in devising the algorithms. Some techniques are Divide & Conquer, Greedy Technique, and Dynamic Programming etc. We choose these techniques on the basis of our problem requirement.

(*b*) ***Write (implementation):*** We can implement an algorithm with the help of any programming language in the form of pseudo code. At the phase of implementation software developers write source code for particular problem by using programming language like C, C++, java, etc.

(*c*) ***Test:*** Testing is the phase where an algorithm is being tested by some predefines data or tools for its correctness. If an algorithm gives write output for a valid input then it is said to be correct otherwise it is design again.

(*d*) ***Analyze:*** Estimating the amount of time/space (which are considered to be prime resources) required while executing the algorithm. This phase give calculation for how much space and time required by any algorithm.

Fig. 1.2. Life Cycle of Algorithm

1.7 CORRECTNESS OF ALGORITHMS

An algorithm is said to be **correct** if, for every input instance, it halts with the correct output. An incorrect algorithm might not halt at all on some input instances, or it might halt with an answer other than the desired one.

1.8 TYPES OF ANALYSIS

An algorithm when implemented, uses the computer's primary memory and Central Processing Unit so analysis of algorithm include the amount of resources needed for a particular solution of the problem. The Analysis is done at two stages:

- **Priori Analysis:** Analysis done before implementation.
- **Posteriori Analysis:** Analysis done after implementation.

(*a*) ***Priori Analysis:*** This is the theoretical estimation of resources required. Here the efficiency of the algorithm is checked. If possible the logic of the algorithm can be improved for efficiency. This is done before the implementation of the algorithm on a machine and so it is done independent of any machine/software.

(*b*) ***Posteriori Analysis:*** This Analysis is done after implementing the algorithm on a target machine. It is aimed at determination of actual statistics about algorithm's consumption of time and space requirements (primary memory) in the computer when it is being executed as a program.

1.9 SPECIFICATION OF ALGORITHMS

An algorithm can be specified in English, as a computer program, or even as a hardware design. The only requirement is that the specification must provide a precise description of the computational procedure to be followed. When issues of control need to be made perfectly clear, we often use ***pseudo code.*** Pseudo code is similar to C, C++, Pascal, and Java. If you know any of these languages, you should be able to understand pseudo code. Pseudo code is designed for expressing algorithms to humans. Software engineering issues of data abstraction, modularity, and error handling are often ignored. We sometimes embed English statements into pseudo code. Therefore, unlike for "real" programming languages, we cannot create a compiler that translates pseudo code to machine code.

Example of pseudo code: An algorithm is independent of any language or machine whereas a program is dependent on a language and machine, to fill the gap between these two, we need pseudo codes. ***Pseudo code*** is a way to represent the step by step methods in finding the solution to the given problem.

Example:

```
Algorithm array // To find maximum of an array//
    Algorithm arrayS(A,n)
    Maxiumum=A[0]
    for i = 1 to n do
       if A[i]>Maximum then
       Maximum = A[i]
    return Maximum
```

Algorithms are developed during the ***design phase*** of software engineering. During the design phase, we first look at the problem, try to write the ***"pseudo code"*** and move towards the programming (implementation) phase. Pseudo-code has following characteristics.

- It is a high level description of the algorithm
- It is less detailed than the program
- It will not reveal the design issues of the program
- Uses statement like English language

1.10 PERFORMANCE MEASURES

Since most of the software problems do not have a unique solution, we are always interested in finding the better solution. A better solution is judged based on its performance. Some of the performance measures include the time taken by the solution, the quality of the solution, the simplicity of the solution, etc. For any solution to a problem we would always ask the following questions: *"Is it feasible to use this solution*?" In other words is it efficient enough to be used in practice? The efficiency measure which we normally look for is time and space.

How much time does this solution take?

How much space (memory) does this solution occupy?

Improving the performance of a solution can be done by improving the algorithm design, database design, and transaction design and by paying attention to the end-user psychology. Also continuous improvements in hardware and communication infrastructure aid in improving the performance of a solution. To measure the performance of an algorithm we emphasise on following criterion:

- Input Classes
- Space Complexity
- Time Complexity

1.10.1 Input Classes

Input is very important for analyzing the algorithm because on the basis of input we can find path of execution of an algorithm. For example, if we are intrested in finding the largest value in a list of N numbers, we can use the following algorithm:

```
Algorithm Largest // To find largest among
array element//
            Largest=S[1]
            For i=2 to n do
                If (S[i]> largest) then
                    Largest=S[i]
             End if
            End for
```

We can see if the array S[] is in decreasing order, there will be only one assignment done before the loop starts. If the is increasing order, however there will be N assignments (one before the loop starts and N-1 inside the loop). Our analysis must contain more than one possible set of input, because if we look at one set of input, it may be the set that is solved fastest or slowest. This will give us a false impression of the algorithm.

1.10.2 Space Complexity

Space complexity is defined as the amount of memory a program needs to run to completion. Why is this of concern?

- We could be running on a multi-user system where programs are allocated a specific amount of space.
- We may not have sufficient memory on our computer.
- There may be multiple solutions, each having different space requirements.
- The space complexity may define an upper bound on the data that the program can handle.

Components of Program Space

Program space = Instruction space + Environment stack space + Data space

Instruction space: is dependent on several factors.

- The compiler that generates the machine code.
- The target computer.

Environment Stack Space: needed when functions are called. If the function, **A** calls another function **B** then the return address and all the local variables and formal parameters are stored. Every time a function is called, the following data are saved on the stack.

- The return address.
- The values of all local variables and value formal parameters.
- The binding of all reference and const reference parameters.

Data space: is dependent on several factors

- Very much dependent on the computer architecture and compiler.
- The magnitude of the data that a program works with is another factor.

Example:

Table 1.1: Space Occupancy

Type	*Capacity*	*Type*	*Capacity (in byte)*
char	1	float	4
short	2	double	8
int	2	long double	10
long	4	pointer	2

Note:

- Choosing a "smaller" data type has an effect on the overall space usage by the Program
- Choosing the correct type is especially important when working with arrays.

Some points for efficient space utilization:

- Always choose the optimal (smallest necessary) data type.
- Study the compiler.
- Learn about the effects of different compilation settings.
- Choose non-recursive algorithms when appropriate.

1.10.3 Time Complexity

Time complexity also depends on all the factors that the space complexity depends on. It includes the compilation time and execution time but compilation is done once whereas the execution is done *n* number of times. So the compilation time is not considered in most of the cases but only the execution time. we should care about time complexity because:

- Some computers require upper limits for program execution times.
- Some program requires a real time response.
- If there are many solutions to a problem, typically we'd like to choose the quickest.

We can measure time complexity by two ways:

1. **Operation counts:** Count a particular operation. The success of this method operation count) depends on the identification of the exact operation/s that contributes most to the time complexity.

   Example:

   - Searching an array for the presence of an element, here the time complexity is estimated Based on the number of search operations.

- Finding the roots of a quadratic equation $ax^2 + bx + c = 0$. The roots are $(-b + \text{sqrt}(b^2 - *a*c))\ 2a$ and $(-b - \text{sqrt}(b^2 - 4*a*c))/2a$. Here the number of operations can be reduced by computing the common expression sqrt $(b^2 - 4*a*c)$.

2. **Step count:** Count the number of steps. The operation-count method omits accountinforthe time spent on all but the chosen operation but the step-count method count for all the time spent in all parts of the program. A program step is loosely defined to be a syntactically or semantically meaningful segment of a program for which the execution time is independent of theinstance Characteristics.100 adds, 100 subtracts, 1000 multiples can be counted as one step.

   However, n adds cannot be counted as one step. For example:

steps/execution	(s/e)
Algorithm Sum(a,n)	0
{	0
s:=0.0;	1
for i=1 to n do	1
s:= s+ a[i];	1
return s;	1
}	

3. **Frequency count:** The step execution does not give exact view that how much time a program need to run that's why we emphasize on frequency execution instead of step count. For example:

	s/e	Frequency
Algorithm Sum(a,n)	0	0
{	0	0
s:=0.0;	1	1
for i=1 to n do	1	n+1
s:= s+ a[i];	1	n
return s;	1	1
}	0	0

Total step counts

= 0+0+1+(n+1)+n+1+0

= 2n + 3

1.11 SHORTCOMINGS OF EMPIRICAL METRICS

Since algorithms are platform-independent (*i.e.,* a given algorithm can be implemented in an arbitrary programming language on an arbitrary computer running an arbitrary operating system), there are significant drawbacks to using an empirical approach to language the comparative performance of a given set of algorithms. Take as an example a program that looks up a specific entry in a sorted list of size *n*. Suppose this program were implemented on Computer A, a state-of-the-art machine, using a linear search algorithm, and on Computer B, a much slower machine, using a binary search algorithm. Benchmark testing on the two computers running their respective programs might look something like the following:

Table 1.2 : Run Time for Different Computers

n (list size)	*Computer A run-time (in nanoseconds)*	*Computer B run-time (in nanoseconds)*
15	7 ns	100,000 ns
65	32 ns	150,000 ns
250	128 ns	200,000 ns
1,000	500 ns	250,000 ns

Based on these metrics, it would be easy to jump to the conclusion that Computer A is running an algorithm that is far superior in efficiency to what Computer B is running. However, if the size of the input-list is increased to a sufficient number, that conclusion is dramatically demonstrated to be in error:

Table 1.3 : Run Time for Different Computers

n (list size)	*Computer A run-time (in nanoseconds)*	*Computer B run-time (in nanoseconds)*
15	7 ns	100,000 ns
65	32 ns	150,000 ns
250	125 ns	200,000 ns
1,000	500 ns	250,000 ns
...	...	...
1,000,000	500,000 ns	500,000 ns
4,000,000	2,000,000 ns	550,000 ns
16,000,000	8,000,000 ns	600,000 ns
...	...	...
$63{,}072 \times 10^{12}$	$31{,}536 \times 10^{12}$ ns, or 1 year	1,375,000 ns, or 1.375 milliseconds

Computer A, running the linear search program, exhibits a linear growth rate. The program's run-time is directly proportional to its input size. Doubling the input size doubles the run time, quadrupling the input size quadruples the run-time, and so forth. Whereas Computer B, running the binary search program, exhibits a logarithmic growth rate. Doubling the input size only increases the run time by a constant amount (in this example, 25,000 ns). Even though Computer A is ostensibly a faster machine, Computer B will inevitably surpass Computer A in run-time because it's running an algorithm with a much slower growth rate.

1.12 MODEL OF COMPUTATION

Model of computation is the definition of the set of allowable operations used in computation and heir respective costs. Only assuming a certain model of computation is it possible to analyze the computational resources required, such as the execution time or memory space or to discuss the limitations of algorithms or computers. In the field of run-time analysis of algorithms, it is common to specify a computational model in terms of primitive operations allowed which have unit cost, or simply unit-cost operations. A commonly used example is the **random access machine**, which has unit cost for read and writes access to all of its memory cells.

The simplest model of computation is a **finite automaton**. In a sense finite automata model every conceivable device, but in a very inefficient way. A fixed finite automaton, when used on inputs of arbitrary size, can compute only very primitive functions, and is not an adequate computation model in itself.

Historically, the first "infinite" model of computation was the **Turing machine**, introduced by the English mathematician A. Turing in 1936, before the invention of programmable computers. This model can be thought of as a finite automaton (control unit) equipped with an infinite storage (memory). More exactly, the memory is an infinite one-dimensional array of cells. The control unit can make arbitrary local changes to the scanned memory cell and change the scanned position by one step.

The most important weakness of the Turing machine in comparison real computers is that its memory is not accessible immediately: in order to read a distant memory cell, all intermediate cells must also be read. This is remedied by the notion of a **Random Access Machine (RAM).** The RAM can reach an arbitrary memory cell in a single step. It can be considered a simplified model of real world computers, along with the abstraction that it has unbounded memory and the capability to store arbitrarily large integers in each of its memory cells. The RAM can be programmed in some specified but arbitrary programming language. For the description of algorithms, it is practical to use the RAM since this is closest to real program writing. But we will see that the Turing machine and the RAM are equivalent from many points of view; what is most important, the same functions are computable on Turing machines and on the RAM.

Unfortunately, these nice properties of the RAM machine come at a cost: in order to be able to read a memory register immediately, we must address it; the address must be stored in another register. Since the number of memory registers is not bounded, the address is not bounded either, and therefore we must allow an arbitrarily large number in the register containing the address. The content of this register must itself change during the running of the program (indirect addressing). This further increases the power of the RAM.

SUMMARY

An algorithm is the step-by-step solution to a certain problem. Algorithm works on five properties:Finiteness, Effectiveness, Definiteness, Input, and Output. There are various classifications of algorithms but not on any particular strategy. Algorithm works in a life cycle which contain four phase: Design, Write, Test and Analysis. We can analyze an algorithm on in two phase –Priori Analysis: Analysis done before implementation. Posteriori Analysis: Analysis done after implementation. To measure the performance of an algorithm we emphasize on fallowing criterion:

- Input Classes
- Space Complexity
- Time Complexity

EXERCISE

1. What do you mean by algorithm? Give any two real life examples where you use algorithm to perform task.
2. Design algorithm for Fibonacci and Factorial program and calculate its step count and frequency count?
3. Define:
   (*a*) Time Efficiency (*b*) Space Efficiency
4. Explain the Algorithm design and analysis process with a neat diagram.
5. What are the important types of problems that encounter in the area of computing?
6. Explain Consecutive Integer Checking algorithm to find the GCD of two numbers with an example.
7. Write a note on measuring the input size of an algorithm.
8. Briefly discuss the Algorithm Analysis Framework.
9. What are different ways of measuring the running time of an algorithm?
10. Give an algorithm to find the smallest element in a list of n numbers and analyze the efficiency.
11. Give an algorithm to check whether all the elements in a list are unique or not and analyze the efficiency.
12. Give an algorithm to multiply two matrices of order N * N and analyze the efficiency.
13. Give the general plan for analyzing the efficiency of Recursive algorithms with an eg.
14. Give an algorithm to compute the Factorial of a positive integer n and analyze the efficiency.
15. Give an algorithm to solve the Tower of Hanoi puzzle and analyze the efficiency.
16. Define an explicit formula for the nth Fibonacci number.
17. With the help of a flowchart, explain the various stages of algorithm design process.
18. Explain any three fundamental problem types.

Chapter 2 GROWTH ORDER

2.1 ANALYSIS OF ALGORITHM

The analysis of the algorithm can be performed based on the nature of the problem. Thus, we have:

- Worst case analysis
- Average case analysis
- Best case analysis

Worst case: Under what condition the algorithm when executed does consumes maximum amount of resources, or in other words we can say it is the maximum amount of resource the algorithm can consume for any value of problem size. In most of the case we prefer worst case analysis.

Best case: Under what conditions the algorithm when executed does consumes minimum amount of resources.

Average case: This is between worst case and best case. It is probabilistic in nature. Average-case running times are calculated by first arriving at an understanding of the average nature of the input, and then performing a running-time analysis of the algorithm for this configuration. Average case analysis is done by considering every possibility is equally likely to happen.

2.2 WHY WORST CASE ANALYSIS?

Even though the average case is more tends towards the real situation worst case analysis is preferred due to the following reasons:

- It is better to bound ones pessimism—the time of execution can't go beyond T(n) as it is the upper bound
- Generally it is easy to compute the worst case analysis as compared to computation of best case and average case of algorithms during Priori analysis.

2.3 PROBLEM SIZE

The problem size depends on the nature of the problem for which we are developing the algorithms. The complexity of an algorithm is expressed as a function of problem size. For example, if we are searching an element in an array having *'n'* elements, the problem size is same as the size of array (=*'n'*). If we are merging 2 arrays of size *'n'* and *'m'*, the problem size of the algorithm is sum of two array sizes (= *'n + m'*). If we are computing the nth factorial, the problem size is *'n'*.

2.4 ORDER OF AN ALGORITHM

Calculate the running time and consider only the leading term of the formula which gives the order of magnitude.

Example 1

```
for( i = 0; i< n; i ++)
{
...
...
}
```

Assume there is *'c'* number of statements inside the loop each statement takes 1 unit of time

Execution time for 1 loop = $c * 1 = c$

Total execution time = $n * c$

Since *'c'* is constant it is insignificant. So **the order is 'n'**

In calculating the order of magnitude, the lower order terms are left out as they are relatively insignificant. The assumptions in the example are made because we will not know on which machine the algorithm is to be implemented. So, we can't exactly say how much time each statement will take. The exact time depends on the machine on which the algorithm is run. In the example the approximation is done because for higher values of *'n'*, the effect of *'c'* (constant) will not be significant. Thus, constants can be ignored.

Example 2

```
for( i=0;i<n; i ++)
{
for(j=0;j<m;j++)
{
.... ....
}
}
```

Assume we have *'c'* number of statements inside the innermost loop then following the same assumptions as the earlier example:

Execution time for 1 loop = $c * 1$

Execution time for the inner loop = $m * c$

Total execution time = $n * (m * c)$

Since c is a constant, the **total execution time = n * m**

In the above example, the inner loop will be executed m times and the outer loop n times.

Recall that the running time of an algorithm is specified as a function of its input size. In general, we want to know the growth rate of individual algorithms and compare the running times of different algorithms. In this part we will introduce some mathematical tools which help us to specify the growth rate of individual algorithms and compare their growth rates. Suppose that we have two algorithms (A and B) for solving the same problem, further that the running times of the algorithms A and B are given by the following functions:

— $TA(n) = n^2 + 6n$

— $TB(n) = 10n + 20$

And now we want to ***compare*** the running times of these algorithms. How can we do it? Can we use any mathematical notation that we already know? Can we use the ">" symbol? That is, is it useful to say that "TA(n) > TB(n)"? It is not because, first of all, it is not true for all values of n. When n is small "TA(n) < TB(n)." But even if it were true it would not be useful. For example, suppose that

— $TA(n) = 10n + 5$

— $TB(n) = 3n + 2$

Now, for all values of n it is true that "TA(n) > TB(n)." It would not be useful because what we need is to compare the ***growth rate*** of functions. The functions $TA(n) = 10n + 5$ and $TB(n) = 3n + 2$ grow at the same rate even though TA(n) > TB(n), Which means that the running times of these two algorithms do not much differ as the input size grows. But if the running time functions of two algorithms have different growth rates than their performance significantly changes as the input size grows. So, we need some special symbols for comparing the growth rate of functions.

Table 2.1: Input Size and Basic Operation Examples

Problem	*Input size measure*	*Basic operation*
Searching for key in a list of n items	Number of list's items, *i.e.*, n	Key comparison
Multiplication of two matrices	Matrix dimensions or total number of elements	Multiplication of two numbers
Checking primality of a given integer n	n'size = number of digits (in binary representation)	Division
Typical graph problem	vertices and/or edges	Visiting a vertex or traversing an edge

Table 2.2: Growth Order Table

log n	*n*	*nlogn*	n^2	n^3	2^n
0	1	0	1	1	2
1	2	2	4	8	4
2	4	8	16	64	16
3	8	24	64	512	256
4	16	64	256	4096	65536
5	32	160	1024	32768	4294967296

2.5 ASYMPTOTIC COMPLEXITY

Asymptotic means a line that tends to converge to a curve, which may or may not eventually touch the curve. It is a line that stays within bounds. **Asymptotic complexity** provides meaningful statements about the time and space complexities of a program. To show asymptotic complexity of algorithm we use various notations known as asymptotic notations. **Asymptotic notation** is a shorthand way to write down and talk about 'fastest possible' and 'slowest possible' running time for an algorithm, using high and low bounds on speed. These are also referred as 'best case' and 'worst case' scenario respectively.

2.6 WHY ARE ASYMPTOTIC NOTATIONS IMPORTANT?

- They give a simple characterization of an algorithm's efficiency.
- They allow the comparison of the performances of various algorithms.
- For large values of components/inputs, the multiplicative constants and lower order terms of an exact *running time* are dominated by the effects of the input size (the number of components).

Table 2.3: Different Asymptotic Notation

S.No.	*Notation*	*Condition*	*Symbol*	*Read as*
1	O	Asymptotic upper bound	≤	Big Oh
2	Ω	Asymptotic lower bound	≤	Big Omega
3	Θ	Asymptotic tight bound	=	Theta
4	o	upper bound that is not aymptotically tight	<	Small Oh
5	ω	lower bound that is not asymptotically tight	>	Small Omega

2.6.1 Big Oh Notation

In 1892, P. Bachmann invented a notation for characterizing the asymptotic behaviour of functions. His invention has come to be known as *big oh notation*: Big-oh is the formal method of expressing the upper bound (Worst Case) of an algorithm's running time. It is the measure of the longest amount of time it could possibly take for the algorithm to complete. In other words we can say it shows the worst case analysis of algorithm. For function $g(n)$, we define $O(g(n))$, big-O of n, as the set as

$$O(g(n)) = \{f(n) : \exists \text{ positive constants } c \text{ and } n_0, \text{ such that } \forall\ n_0, \text{ we have } 0 \le f(n) \le cg(n)\}$$

Intuitively: Set of all functions whose *rate of growth* is the same as or lower than that of $g(n)$.

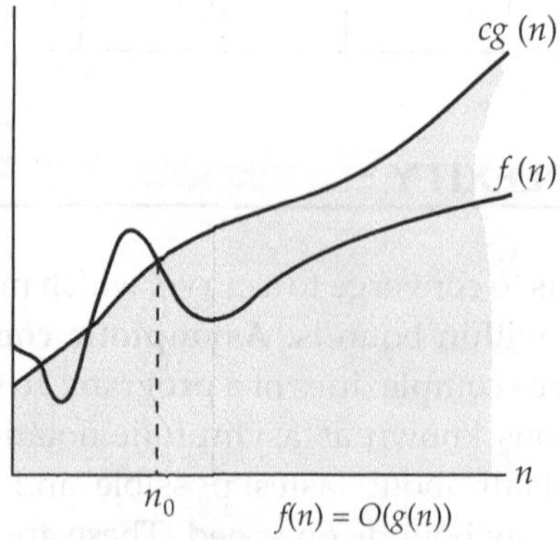

Fig. 2.1. Graph of Big. Oh Notation

Example:

1. $T(n) = 2n + 5$ is $O(n)$. Why?

$2n + 5 <= 3n$, {put the value of n like (0,1,2,3,4.......)

for all **n** > = 5

2. $T(n) = 5*n^2 + 3*n + 15$ is $O(n^2)$. Why?

$5*n^2 + 3*n + 15 <= 6*n^2$, for all $n >= 6$

3. $2n^2 = O(n^3)$:

$2n^2 \le n^3 \Rightarrow \le cn$, for all $n >= 2$

2.6.2 Big Omega Notation

Big-Omega is the formal method of expressing the lower bound (Best Case) of an algorithm's running time. It is the measure of the smallest amount of time it could possibly take for the algorithm to complete. In other words we can say it shows the best case analysis of algorithm. For function $g(n)$, we define $\Omega(g(n))$, big-Omega of n, as the set as:

$\Omega(g(n)) = \{f(n)\ \exists$ positive constants c and n_0, such that $\forall\ n \geq n_0$, we have $0 \leq cg(n) \leq f(n)\}$

Intuitively: Set of all functions whose *rate of growth* is the same as or higher than that of $g(n)$.

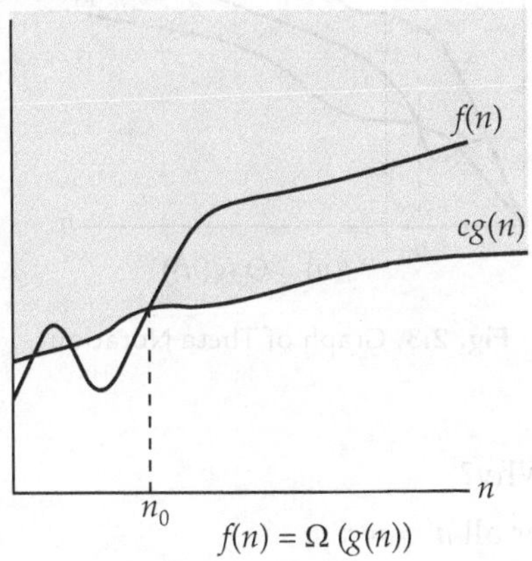

Fig. 2.2. Graph of Big-Omega Notation

Example:

1. $T(n) = 2n + 5$ is $\Omega(n)$. Why?

$2n + 5 >= 2n,$

for all $n >= 1$

2. $T(n) = 5*n^2 + 3*n + 15$ is $\Omega(n^2)$. Why?

$5*n^2 + 3*n + 15 >= 5*n^2$, for all $n >= 1$

3. $2n^2 = \Omega(n^3)$:

$2n^2 >= n^3 \Rightarrow 2 >= cn$, for all $n >= 1$

2.6.3 Theta Notation

Theta is the formal method of expressing the tight bound (Average Case) of an algorithm's running time. It is the measure of the average amount of time it could possibly take for the algorithm to complete. In other words we can say it shows the average case analysis of algorithm. For function $g(n)$, we define $\Theta(g(n))$, big-theta of n, as the set as:

$\Theta(g(n)) = \{f(n)\ \exists$ positive constants c and n_0, such that $\forall n \geq n_0$, we have $0 \leq c_1 g(n) \leq f(n) \leq c_2 g(n)\}$

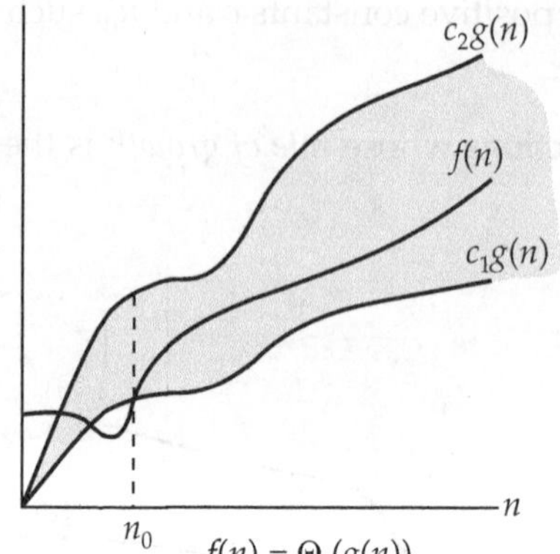

$f(n) = \Theta\ (g(n))$

Fig. 2.3. Graph of Theta Notation

Example:

1. $T(n) = 2n + 5$ is $Q(n)$. Why?

   $2n <= 2n + 5 <= 3n$, for all $n >= 5$

2. $T(n) = 5{*}n_2 - 3{*}\ n$ is $Q(n_2)$. Why?

   $4{*}n_2 <= 5{*}n_2 - 3{*}n <= 5{*}n_2$, for all $n >= 4$

2.6.4 Little Oh Notation

Little Oh is the formal method of expressing the upper bound but not asymptotically tight bound of an algorithm's running time. It is the measure of the approximate worst amount of time it could possibly take for the algorithm to complete.

For a given function $g(n)$, the set little-o:

$$o(g(n)) = \{f(n): \forall\ c > 0, \exists\ n_0 > 0 \text{ such that } \forall\ n \geq n_0, \text{ we have } 0 \leq f(n) < cg(n)\}.$$

$f(n)$ becomes insignificant relative to $g(n)$ as n approaches infinity:

$$\lim_{n \to \infty} [f(n)/g(n)] = 0$$

$g(n)$ is an ***upper bound*** for $f(n)$ that is not asymptotically tight.

2.6.5 Little Omega Notation

Little Omega is the formal method of expressing the lower bound but not asymptotically tight bound of an algorithm's running time. It is the measure of the approximate fastest amount of time it could possibly take for the algorithm to complete.

For a given function $g(n)$, the set little-o:

$$o(g(n)) = \{f(n): \forall\ c > 0, \exists\ n_0 > 0 \text{ such that } \forall\ n \leq n_0, \text{ we have } 0\ cg(n) < f(n)\}.$$

$f(n)$ becomes insignificant relative to $g(n)$ as n approaches infinity:

$$\lim_{n \to \infty} [f(n)/g(n)] = \infty$$

$g(n)$ is an *upper bound* for $f(n)$ that is not asymptotically tight.

2.6.6 Big 'Oh' Vs Big 'Omega' Notations

Case I: A project manager requires maximum of 100 software engineers to finish the project on time.

Case II: The Project manager can start the project with minimum of 50 software engineers but cannot assure the completion of project in time.

Case I: is similar to Big Oh notation, specifying the upper bound of resources needed to do a task.

Case II: is similar to Omega notation, specifying the lower bound of resources needed to do a task

Which case is preferred?

Case (I) is preferred in most of the situations.

2.6.7 'Big Oh' Manipulations

While finding the worst case complexities of algorithms using Big Oh notation, some/all of the following rules are used.

Rule I: The leading coefficients of highest power of 'n' and all lower powers of 'n' is considered and the constants are ignored in $f(n)$

Example:

$T(n) = O(100n^3 + 29n^2 + 19n)$ Representing the same in big Oh notation $T(n) = O(n^3)$

The constants and the slower growing terms are ignored as their growth rates are insignificant compared to the growth rate of the highest power.

Rule II: The time of execution of a 'for loop' is the 'running time' of all statements inside the 'for loop' multiplied by number of iterations of the 'for loop'.

Example:

```
For (i=0 to n)
{
    x=x+1;
    y=y+1;
    x=x+y
}
```

The 'for loop' is executed n times. So, worst case running time of the algorithm is

$$T(n) = O(3^*n) = O(n)$$

Rule III: If we have a 'nested for loop', in an algorithm, the analysis of that algorithm should start from the inner loop and move it outwards towards outer loop.

Example:

```
For (j=0 to m)
{
    For (i=0 to n)
    {
    x = x + 1;
    y = y + 1;
    z = x + y;
    }
}
```

The worst case running time of inner loop is $O(3 * n)$

The worst case running time of outer loop is $O(m * 3 * n)$

The total running time = $O(m * n)$

Rule IV: The execution of an 'if else statement' is an algorithm comprises of execution time for testing the condition and the maximum execution time of either '*if*' or 'else'(whichever is larger)

Example:

```
If(x>y)
{
    Print("x is larger than y");
    Print("x is the value to be selected");
    z=x;
    x=x+1;
}
```

Else

Print ("x is smaller than y");

The execution time of the program is the execution time of testing (X > Y) + execution time of '*if*' statement, as the execution time of 'if' statement is more than that of 'else' statement

All sorting algorithms are $\Omega(n\lg(n))$

Given a list of n items, there are $n!$ possible arrangements of these items. Let each one of these arrangements be a leaf in a binary tree with the original arrangement as the root. Then the height of this (balanced) binary tree is $lg(n!)$ and we have just seen that this function is $\Omega(nlg(n))$.

The length of the path from the root to any one of the leaves can be no shorter than a constant multiple of $nlg(n)$ and no comparison sorting algorithm can do better than this number of compares. Note we use the weaker claim that $lg(n!) = \Omega(nlg(n))$ rather than the stronger statement that it is $\Theta(nlog(n))$ because no comparison sorting algorithm can do better than the minimum number of compares to go from the root to the appropriate leaf of the sorting tree, but not all sorting algorithms will be this efficient.

Sorting Tree for a list of Size 3

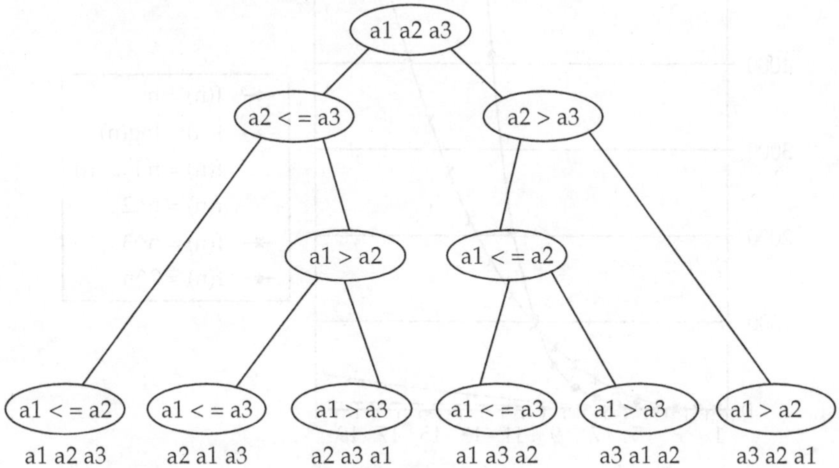

Fig. 2.4. Representing Sorting Tree

2.6.8 Running Time and Asymptotic Notation

The running time is $O(n^2) \rightarrow$ not asymptotically slower than n^2 for any inputs.

The running time is $\Omega(n^2) \rightarrow$ not asymptotically faster than n^2 for any inputs.

The running time is $\Theta(n^2) \rightarrow$ asymptotically equal to n^2 for any inputs.

2.7 TYPICAL RUNNING TIME FUNCTIONS

Run time of the following time functions are given as follows:

1 (constant running time): Instructions are executed once or a few times

logN (logarithmic): A big problem is solved by cutting the original problem in smaller Size, by a constant fraction at each step

N (linear): A small amount of processing is done on each input element

N logN: A problem is solved by dividing it into smaller problems, solving them independently and combining the solution

N^2 (quadratic): Typical for algorithms that process all pairs of data items (double nested loops)

N^3 (cubic): Processing of triples of data (triple nested loops)

N^K (polynomial):

2^n (exponential): Few exponential algorithms are appropriate for practical use.

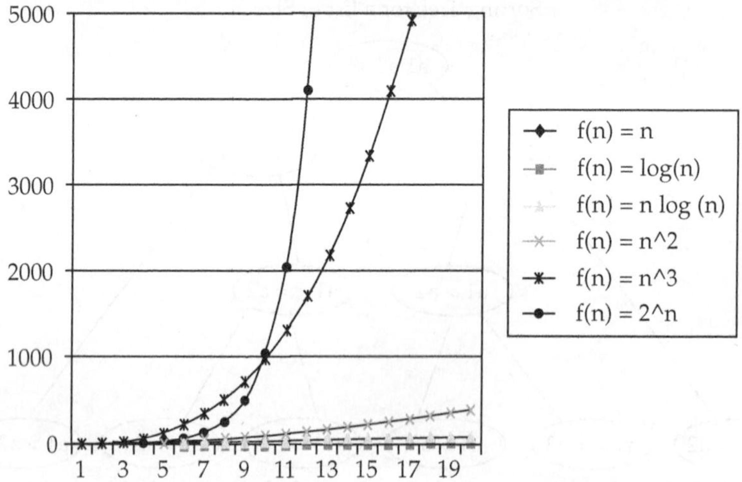

Fig. 2.5. Graph Representation of Running Time Function

2.8 LIMIT

Another useful way to compare the growth rate of functions is to use limit as follows (and use the L'Hopital's rule when necessary)

$$L = \lim_{n \to \infty} \frac{f(n)}{g(n)}$$

L'Hopital's rule when necessary)

- If $L = 0$ then $f(n) = o(g(n))$
- If $L = \infty$ then $f(n) = \omega(g(n))$
- If $L = c$ then $f(n) = \Theta(g(n))$
- If $0 \leq L < \infty$ then $f(n) = O(g(n))$
- If $0 < \leq \infty$ then $f(n) = \Omega(g(n))$

2.9 PROPERTIES OF ASYMPTOTIC NOTATIONS

1. **Transitivity:**

   If $f(n) = Q(g(n))$ and $g(n) = Q(h(n))$ then $f(n) = Q(h(n))$.

   If $f(n) = O(g(n))$ and $g(n) = O(h(n))$ then $f(n) = O(h(n))$.

   If $f(n) = W(g(n))$ and $g(n) = W(h(n))$ then $f(n) = W(h(n))$.

   If $f(n) = o(g(n))$ and $g(n) = o(h(n))$ then $f(n) = o(h(n))$.

   If $f(n) = w(g(n))$ and $g(n) = w(h(n))$ then $f(n) = w(h(n))$.

2. **Reflexivity:**

   $$f(n) = Q(f(n)).$$
   $$f(n) = O(f(n)).$$
   $$f(n) = W(f(n)).$$

   "o" is not reflexive

   "ω" is not reflexive

3. **Symmetry and Transpose symmetry:**
   - **Symmetry:**

     $$f(n) = Q(g(n)) \text{ if and only if } g(n) = Q(f(n)).$$

   - **Transpose symmetry:**

     $$f(n) = O(g(n)) \text{ if and only if } g(n) = W(f(n)).$$
     $$f(n) = o(g(n)) \text{ if and only if } g(n) = w(f(n)).$$

4. **Analogy between asymptotic comparison of functions and comparison of real numbers.**

   $$f(n) = O(g(n)) \quad » \quad a <= b$$
   $$f(n) = W(g(n)) \quad » \quad a >= b$$
   $$f(n) = Q(g(n)) \quad » \quad a = b$$
   $$f(n) = o(g(n)) \quad » \quad a < b$$
   $$f(n) = w(g(n)) \quad » \quad a > b$$

   f(n) is asymptotically smaller than g(n) if $f(n) = o(g(n))$

   f(n) is asymptotically larger than g(n) if $f(n) = w(g(n))$

5. **Exponentials:** For all real $a > 0$, m, and n, we have the following identities:

   $$a_o = 1,$$
   $$a^1 = a,$$
   $$a^{-1} = 1/a$$
   $$(am)^n = am^n$$
   $$(am)^n = (an)^m$$
   $$a^m a^n = a^{m+n}$$

6. **Logarithms:** In algorithm analysis we often use the notation "log n" without specifying the base

Binary logarithm	$\log n = \log_2 n$
Natural Number	$\log n = \log_e n$

Some Logrithmic formulas

$$\log^k n = (\log n)^k$$

$$\log\log n = \log(\log n)$$

$$\log x^y = y \log x$$

$$\log xy = \log x + \log y$$

$$\log x/y = \log x - \log y$$

$$\log_a x = \log_a b \log_b x$$

$$a^{\log_b x} = x^{\log_b a}$$

7. **Theorem**

$$A(n) = a_m n^m + a_{m-1} n^{m-1} + \ldots + a_1 n + a_0$$

a polynominal of degree $m,^{n,m\geq 0}$ for all $i,^{a_i \in R}$

To Prove: $A(n) = O(n^m) = a_m n^m + O(n^{m-1})$

Example: $5n^3 + 2n^2 - 5 - O(n^3) - 5n^3 + O(n^2)$

Proof:

To Prove: $| A(n) \leq c \mid n^m \mid$

$$| A(n) | \leq | a_m | n^m + | a_{m-1} | n^{m-1} + \ldots + | a_1 | n + | a_0 |$$

$$\leq n^m \left(| a_m | + \left| \frac{a_{m-1}}{n} \right| + \ldots + \frac{| a_1 |}{n^{m-1}} + \frac{) a_1 |}{n^m} \right)$$

$$\leq n^m (| a_m | + | a_{m-1} | + \ldots + | a_0 |)$$

$$c = | a_m | + | a_{m-1} | + \ldots + | a_0 |$$

$$n_o = 1$$

2.10 SOME PRACTICAL FACTS

When comparing the growth rate of functions you can use the following practical facts:

- Exponential functions grow faster than polynomial functions which grow faster than logarithmic functions.
- The base of a logarithm doesn't matter asymptotically, but the base of an exponential and the degree of a polynomial do matter.

SUMMARY

Asymptotic analysis is based on the idea that as the problem size grows, the complexity will eventually settle down to a simple proportionality to some known function. This idea is incorporated in the "Big Oh" "Big Omega" and "Big Theta" notation for asymptotic performance. These notations are useful for expressing the complexity of an algorithm without getting lost in unnecessary detail. Speaking very roughly, "Big Oh" relates to an upper bound on complexity, "Big Omega" relates to a lower bound, and "Big Theta" relates to a tight bound. While the "bound" idea may help us develop an intuitive understanding of complexity.

EXERCISE

1. For each of the following pairs of functions, either $f(n)$ is $O(g(n))$, $f(n)$ is $\Omega(g(n))$, or $f(n)$ is $\Theta(g(n))$. Determine which relationship is correct.
   - $f(n) = \log n_2; g(n) = \log n + 5$
   - $f(n) = n; g(n) = \log n_2$
   - $f(n) = \log \log n; g(n) = \log n$
   - $f(n) = n; g(n) = \log_2 n$
   - $f(n) = n \log n + n; g(n) = \log n$
   - $f(n) = 10; g(n) = \log_{10}$
   - $f(n) = 2n; g(n) = 10n_2$
   - $f(n) = 2n; g(n) = 3n$
2. Is $2n = O(n!)$?

   Is $2n = \Theta(n!)$?

   Is $2n = o(n!)$?
3. Define different constraints in algorithm to find out complexity?
4. Arrange the following growth rate in the increasing order

   $O(n^3)$,$O(1)$, $O(n^2)$,$O(nlogn)$,$O(n^2logn)$, $\Omega(n^{0.5})$, $\Omega(nlog\ n)$, $\Theta(n^3)$, $\Theta(n^{0.5})$
5. Define following terms:

   (*a*) Big Oh (*b*) Big Omega

   (*c*) Big Theta (*d*) Little Oh

   (*e*) Little Omega.
6. Check for the correctness of following inequalities:

   (*i*) $10n^2 + 4n + 2 = O(n^2)$ (*ii*) $100n + 6 = \Omega(n)$

   (*iii*) $3n + 2 = O(n^2)$ (*iv*) $3n + 3 = \Theta(n)$

   (*v*) $n! = O(n^n)$
7. Show that if C is a +ve real number, then

   $g(n) = 1 + C + C^2 + \ldots\ldots C^n$ is:

   (*i*) $\Theta(1)$ if $c < 1$ (*ii*) $\Theta(n)$ if $c = 1$

   (*iii*) $\Theta(C^n)$ if $c > 1$

Chapter 3 ELEMENTARY DATA STRUCTURE

3.1 DATA STRUCTURE

In computer science, a **data structure** is a particular way of storing and organizing data in a computer so that it can be used efficiently. Different kinds of data structures are suited to different kinds of applications, and some are highly specialized to certain tasks. For example, B-trees are particularly well-suited for implementation of databases, while compiler implementations usually use hash tables to look up identifiers. Data structures are used in almost every program or software system. Specific data structures are essential ingredients of many efficient algorithms, and make possible the management of huge amounts of data, such as large databases and internet indexing services. Some formal design methods and programming languages emphasize data structures, rather than algorithms, as the key organizing factor in software design.

3.2 WHAT THE APPLICATION NEEDS

Terms describing the data structure from the point of view of the application, which only cares how it behaves and not how it is implemented.

List: Generic term for a collection of objects. May or may not contain duplicates. Application may or may not require that it be kept in a specified order.

Ordered-list: List in which the order matters to the application. Therefore, the implementer cannot scramble the order to improve efficiency.

Set: List where the order does not matter to the application (implementer can pick order so as to optimize performance) and in which there are no duplicates.

Multi-set: Like a set, but may contain duplicates.

Double-ended queue (Dequeue): An ordered list in which insertion and deletion occur only at the two ends of the list. That is, elements cannot be inserted into the middle of the list or deleted from the middle of the list.

Stack: An ordered list in which insertion and deletion both occur only at one end (*e.g.* at the start).

Queue: An ordered list in which insertion always occurs at one end and deletion always occurs at the other end.

Linked-list: A linked list is a complex data structure, especially useful in systems or applications programming. A linked list is comprised of a series of nodes, each node containing a data element, and a pointer to the next node.

Tree: Tree is a non-empty collection of vertices & edges that satisfies certain requirements. A vertex is a simple object (node) that can have a name and carry other associated information. An edge is a connection between two vertices.

Graph: Graph is a data structure which is collection of two sets (V, E) which represent vertices and edges. Any two vertices in the graph is connected with the help of an edge. If any of vertices of graph is not connected then graph is not completely connected graph.

3.3 IMPLEMENTATION METHODS

There are a variety of options for the person implementing a list, set, stack or whatever.

Array: We all know what arrays are? Arrays are included here because a list can be implemented using a 1D array. If the maximum length of the list is not known in advance, code must be provided to detect array overflow and expand the array. Expanding requires allocating a new, longer array, copying the contents of the old array, and de-allocating the old array. Arrays are commonly used when two conditions hold. First the maximum length of the list can be accurately estimated in advance (so array expansion is rarely needed). Second, insertion and deletion occur only at the ends of the list. (Insertion and deletion in the middle of an array-based list is slow).

Linked list: A linked list is a data structure which can change during execution. All the successive elements are connected by pointers. Last element of list always points to NULL. Like array we are not bounded to requirement of element, it can grow or shrink in size during execution of a program. It can be made just as long as required. Linked lists are commonly used when the length of the list is not known in advance and/or when it is frequently necessary to insert and/or delete in the middle of the list. Linked lists provide flexibility in allowing the items to be rearranged efficiently.

Doubly-linked list: In a doubly-linked list, each node points to the next node and also to the previous node. In a singly-linked list, each node points to the next node but not back to the previous node. Each node in the doubly list has two pointers, one to the next node and one to the previous one-again, the ends of the list are defined by NULL pointers. Also there is no pointer to the start of the list. Instead, there is simply a pointer to some position in the list which can be moved left or right. The reason we needed a start pointer in the ordinary linked list is because, having moved on from one node to another so without the start pointer, we would lose track of all the nodes in the list that we have already passed. With the doubly linked list, we can move the current pointer backwards and forwards at will.

Circular list: A linked-list is in which the last node points to the first node. If the list is doubly-linked, the first node must also point back to the last node.

Binary tree: Used to implement lists whose elements have a natural order (*e.g.*, numbers) and either (*a*) the application would like the list kept in this order or (*b*) the order of elements is irrelevant to the application (*e.g.*, this list is implementing a set). Each element in a binary tree is stored in a "node" class (or structure). Each node contains pointers to a left child node and a right child node. In some implementations, it may also contain a pointer to the parent node. A tree may also have an object of a second "tree" class (or structure) which as a header for the tree. The "tree" object contains a pointer to the root of the tree (the node with no parent) and whatever other information the programmer wants to squirrel away in it (*e.g.*, number of nodes currently in the tree). In a binary tree, elements are kept sorted in left to right order across the tree. That is, if N is a node, then the value stored in N must be larger than the value stored in left-child (N) and less than the value stored in right-child (N). Variant trees may have the opposite order (smaller values to the right rather than to the left) or may allow two different nodes to contain equal values.

3.4 ABSTRACTED DATA TYPE

The first thing with which one is confronted when writing programs is the *problem*. Typically you are confronted with "real-life" problems and you want to make life easier by providing a program for the problem. However, real-life problems are nebulous and the first thing you have to do is to try to understand the problem to separate necessary from unnecessary details: You try to obtain your own abstract view, or *model*, of the problem. This process of modeling is called *abstraction* and is illustrated in Figure 3.1.

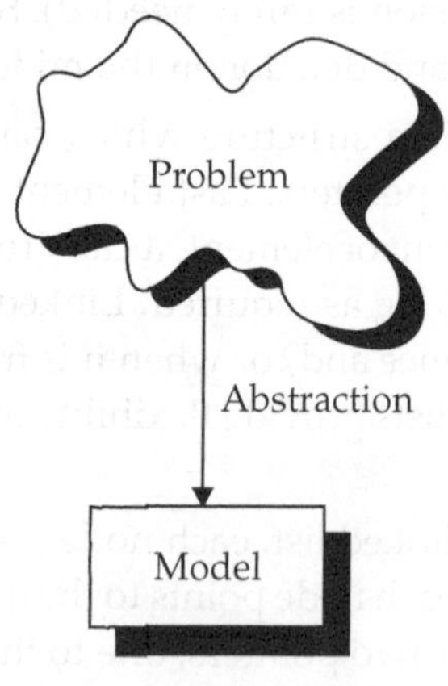

Fig. 3.1. Representing Abstract View of Problem

The model defines an abstract view to the problem. This implies that the model focuses only on problem related stuff and that you try to define properties of the problem. These properties include:

- The *data* which are affected and
- The *operations* which are identified by the problem.

As an example consider the management of student activity in an institution. The head of the administration comes to you and ask you to create a program which allows manage the students.

Well, this is not very specific. For example, what student information is needed by the administration? What tasks should be allowed? Student are real persons who can be characterized with many properties; very few are:

- name,
- sex,
- date of birth,
- Class,
- Enrollment number,
- social number,
- room number,
- hair color,
- hobbies.

Certainly not all of these properties are necessary to solve the administration problem. Only some of them are problem specific. Consequently you create a model of student for the problem. This model only implies properties which are needed to fulfill the requirements of the administration, for instance name, date of birth and social number. These properties are called the *data* of the (student) model. Now, you have described real persons with help of an abstract student. Of course, the pure description is not enough. There must be some operations defined with which the administration is able to handle the abstract student. For example, there must be an operation which allows you to create a new student once a new person enters the institution. Consequently, you have to identify the operations which should be able to be performed on an abstract student. You also decide to allow access to the students' data only with associated operations. This allows you to ensure that data elements are always in a proper state. For example you are able to check if a provided date is valid. To sum up, abstraction is the structuring of a nebulous problem into well-defined entities by defining their data and operations. Consequently, these entities *combine* data and operations. They are **not** decoupled from each other.

3.5 PROPERTIES OF ABSTRACT DATA TYPES

The example of the previous section shows, that with abstraction you create a well-defined entity which can be properly handled. These entities define the *data structure* of a set of items. For example, each managed student has a name, date of birth and social number. The data structure can only be accessed with defined *operations*. This set of operations is called *interface* and is *exported* by the entity. An entity with the properties just described is called an *abstract data type* (ADT). Figure shows an ADT which consists of an abstract data structure and operations. Only the operations are viewable from the outside and define the interface.

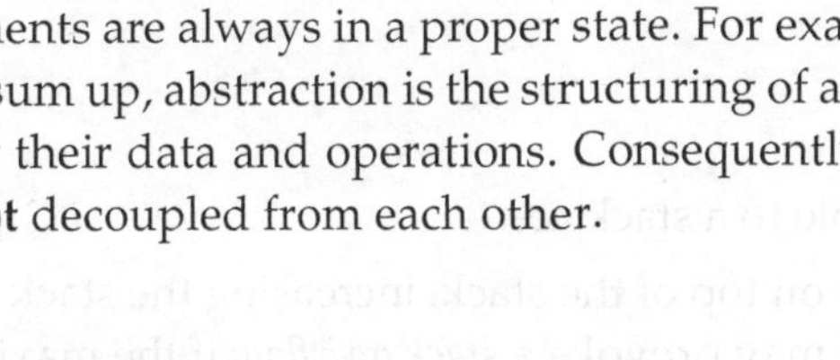

Fig. 3.2. An Abstract Data Type (ADT)

Once a new student is "created" the data structure is filled with actual values: You now have an *instance* of an abstract student. You can create as many instances of an abstract student as needed to describe every real enrolled student. Let's try to put the characteristics of an ADT in a more formal way:

Definition (Abstract Data Type) An **abstract data type** (ADT) is characterized by the following properties:

1. It exports a **type**.
2. It exports a **set of operations**. This set is called **interface**.
3. Operations of the interface are the one and only access mechanism to the type's data structure.
4. Axioms and preconditions define the application domain of the type.

3.6 STACK

A **stack** is a data structure that works on the principle of Last In First Out (LIFO). This means that the last item put on the stack is the first item that can be taken off, like a physical stack of plates. A **stack-based** computer system is one that is based on the use of stacks, rather than being register based.

3.6.1 Operations of Stack

The main operations applicable to a stack are:

- *Push:* An item is put on top of the stack, increasing the stack size by one. As stack size is usually limited, this may provoke a *stack overflow* if the maximum size is exceeded.
- *Pop:* The top item is taken from the stack, decreasing stack size by one. In the case where there was no top item (*i.e.* the stack was empty), a stack underflow occurs.
- *Dup:* The top item is popped and pushed again twice, so that an additional copy of the former top item is now on top, with the original below it.
- *Swap or exchange:* The two topmost items are exchanged.
- *Rotate:* The three topmost items exchange places in a rotary fashion. Two variants of this operation are possible; most often called **left** and **right rotate.**
- *IsEmpty:* Reports whether the stack is empty.
- *IsFull:* Report Whether the stack is full.
- *Initialise:* Create the structure *i.e.*, ensure that the structure exists but contains no elements.

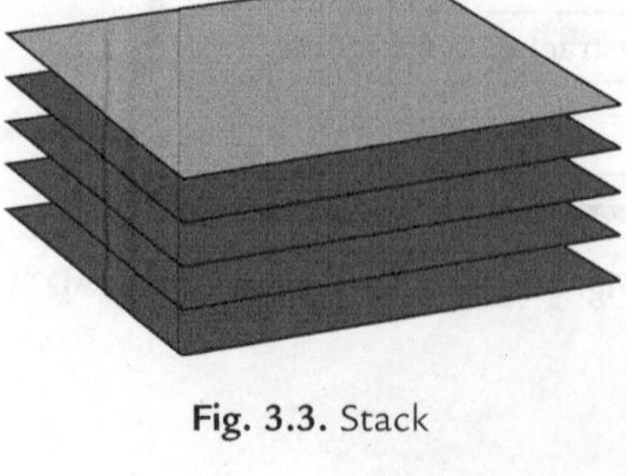

Fig. 3.3. Stack

Stacks are either visualized growing from the bottom up (like real-world stacks, see image) or growing from left to right, so that "topmost" becomes "right most". This means that a **right rotate** will move the first element to the third position, the second to the first and the third to the second. Here are two equivalent visualizations of this process:

Apple banana banana → right rotate → banana banana apple

Cucumber banana apple → right rotate → apple cucumber banana

A stack may be represented in computers inside block of memory cells, with the bottom at a fixed location, and a variable **stack pointer** to the current top cell. **Pushing** first increases the top pointer by one, pointing it to the next cell, and then fills that with the new top value. **Popping** first takes the top value, and then decreases the top pointer by one. Increasing and decreasing may be exchanged to yield a stack representation that grows from high addresses to lower ones.

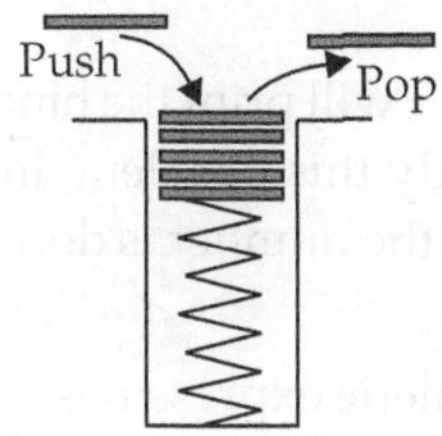

Fig. 3.4. Stack with Push and Pop Operation

3.6.2 Algorithm for Stack Operations

```
Algorithm for push operation

procedure push (item: items);
{add item to the global stack;
top is the current top of stack
and n is its maximum size}
begin
if top=n then stackfull;
top:=top+1;
stack(top):= item;
end: {of push}
```

```
Algorithm for pop operation

procedure pop(var item: items);
{remove top element from the
stack stack and put it in the
item}
begin
if top = 0 then stackempty;
item := stack(top);
top := top-1;
end; {of pop}
```

3.6.3 Stack Applications

1. **Reversing data:** We can use stacks to reverse data example Files, String. By using different operation of stack we can reverse the data. This technique is very useful for finding palindromes. Consider the following pseudo code:

   (*a*) read (data)

   (*b*) loop (data not EOF and stack not full)

(1) push (data)

(2) read (data)

(*c*) loop (while stack notEmpty)

(1) pop (data)

(2) print (data)

2. **Converting decimal to binary:** Consider the following pseudo code

(*a*) Read (number)

(*b*) Loop (number > 0)

(1) digit = number modulo 2

(2) print (digit)

(3) number = number/2

The problem with this code is that it will print the binary number backwards. (ex: 19 becomes 11001000 instead of 00010011.) To remedy this problem, instead of printing the digit right away, we can push it onto the stack. Then after the number is done being converted, we pop the digit out of the stack and print it.

3. **Postponement:** Evaluating arithmetic expressions.

- Prefix: + *a b*
- Infix: *a* + *b* (what we use in grammar school)
- Postfix: *a b* +

In high level languages, infix notation cannot be used to evaluate expressions. We must analyze the expression to determine the order in which we evaluate it. A common technique is used to convert a infix notation into postfix notation, then evaluating it, in which we use stack.

Infix to Postfix Conversion

- Rules:
  - Operands immediately go directly to output
  - Operators are pushed into the stack (including parenthesis)
  - Check to see if stack top operator is less than current operator
  - If the top operator is less than, push the current operator onto stack
  - If the top operator is greater than the current, pop top operator and push onto stack, push current operator onto stack

- Priority 2: */
- Priority 1: + –
- Priority 0: (

If we encounter a right parenthesis, pop from stack until we get matching left parenthesis. Do not output parenthesis. A + B * C – D/E

Infix	*Stack(bot->top)*	*Postfix*
(*a*) A + B * C – D / E		
(*b*) + B * C – D / E		A
(c) B * C – D / E	+	A
(*d*) * C – D / E	+	A B
(*e*) C – D / E	+ *	A B
(*f*) – D / E	+ *	A B C
(*g*) D / E	+ -	A B C *
(*h*) / E	+ -	A B C * D
(*i*) E	+ - /	A B C * D
(*j*)	+ - /	A B C * D E
(*k*)		A B C * D E / – +

4. **Backtracking:** Stacks can be used to backtrack to achieve certain goals. Usually, we set up backtrack tokens to indicate backtrack opportunity.

3.7 QUEUE

Queue is a linear data structure in which data can be added to one end and retrieved from the other. Just like the queue of the real world, the data that goes first into the queue is the first one to be retrieved. That is why queues are sometimes called as **First-In-First-Out** data structure. In case of stack, we saw that data is inserted and deleted both from one end but in case of Queues; data is added to one end (known as REAR) and retrieved from the other end (known as FRONT). The data first added is the last one to be retrieved in stack while in case of queues the data first added is the first one to be retrieved. Two most common terms are used to represent Queue insert and delete end.

1. *Rear:* A variable stores the index number in the array at which the new data will be added (in the queue).
2. *Front:* It is a variable storing the index number in the array where the data will be retrieved.

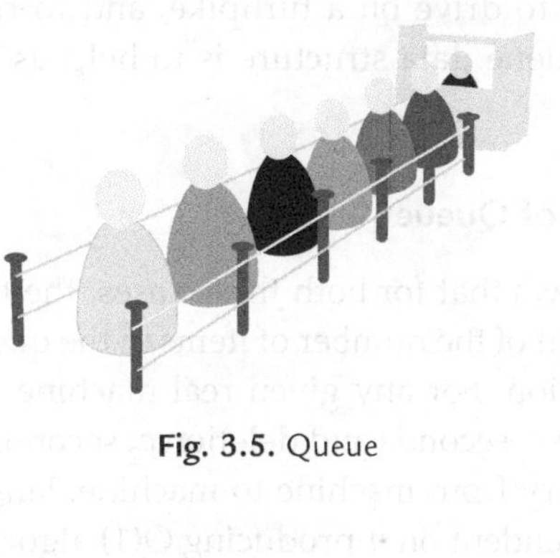

Fig. 3.5. Queue

3.7.1 Operations of Queue

- **Enqueue(x):**insert the element x to the tail of the queue
- **Dequeue():**remove the first element from the head of the queue
- **Top():**check the next element to be removed (do not remove)
- **IsEmpty():**whether the queue is empty

3.7.2 Algorithm for Queue Operation

```
procedure enqueue(item:
items);
{additem to the queue q}
begin
   if rear=n then queuefull
   else begin
      rear :=rear+1;
      q[rear]:=item;
   end;
end;{of enqueue}
```

```
procedure dequeue (varitem:
items);
{delete from the front of q and put
into item}
begin
   if front = rear then queueempty
   else begin
      front:= front+1
      item:=q[front];
   end;
end; {of dequeue}
```

3.7.3 Applications of Queue

Typical uses of queues are in simulations and operating systems.

- Operating systems often maintain a queue of processes that are ready to execute or that are waiting for a particular event to occur.
- Computer systems must often provide a "holding area" for messages between two processes, two programs, or even two systems. This holding area is usually called a "buffer" and is often implemented as a queue.

Our software queues have counterparts in real world queues. We wait in queues to buy pizza, to enter movie theaters, to drive on a turnpike, and to ride on a roller coaster. Another important application of the queue data structure is to help us simulate and analyze such real world queues.

3.7.4 Performance Analysis of Queue

A straightforward analysis shows that for both these cases, the time needed to add or delete an item is constant and independent of the number of items in the queue. Thus we class both addition and deletion as an O(1) operation. For any given real machine + operating system + language combination, addition may take c_1 seconds and deletion c_2 seconds, but we aren't interested in the value of the constant, it will vary from machine to machine, language to language, *etc*. The key point is that the time is not dependent on *n*-producing O(1) algorithms.

Once we have written an O(1) method, there is generally little more that we can do from an algorithmic point of view. Occasionally, a better approach may produce a lower constant time. Often, enhancing our compiler, run-time system, machine, *etc* will produce some significant improvement. However O(1) methods are already very fast, and it's unlikely that effort expended in improving such a method will produce much real gain!

3.7.5 Priority Queues

Often the items added to a queue have a priority associated with them: this priority determines the order in which they exit the queue-highest priority items are removed first.

This situation arises often in process control systems. Imagine the operator's console in a large automated factory. It receives many routine messages from all parts of the system: they are assigned a low priority because they just report the normal functioning of the system—they update various parts of the operator's console display simply so that there is some confirmation that there are no problems. It will make little difference if they are delayed or lost. However, occasionally something breaks or fails and alarm messages are sent. These have high priority because some action is required to fix the problem. Typically such a system will be composed of many small units, one of which will be a buffer for messages received by the operator's console. The communications system places messages in the buffer so that communications links can be freed for further messages while the console software is processing the message. The console software extracts messages from the buffer and updates appropriate parts of the display system. Obviously we want to sort messages on their priority so that we can ensure that the alarms are processed immediately and not delayed behind a few thousand routine messages while the plant is about to explode. As we have seen, we could use a tree structure-which generally provides $O(logn)$ performance for both insertion and deletion. Unfortunately, if the tree becomes unbalanced, performance will degrade to $O(n)$ in pathological cases. This will probably not be acceptable when dealing with dangerous industrial processes, nuclear reactors, flight control systems and other life-critical systems.The array implementation of our collection has one serious drawback: you must know the maximum number of items in your collection when you create it. This presents problems in programs in which this maximum number cannot be predicted accurately when the program starts up. Fortunately, we can use a structure called a linked list to overcome this limitation.

3.8 LINKED LISTS

The linked list is a very flexible dynamic data structure items may be added to it or deleted from it at will. A programmer need not worry about how many items a program will have to accommodate: this allows us to write robust programs which require much less maintenance. A very common source of problems in program maintenance is the need to increase the capacity of a program to handle larger collections: even the most generous allowance for growth tends to prove inadequate over time. In a linked list, each item is allocated space as it is added to the list. A link is kept with each item to the next item in the list.

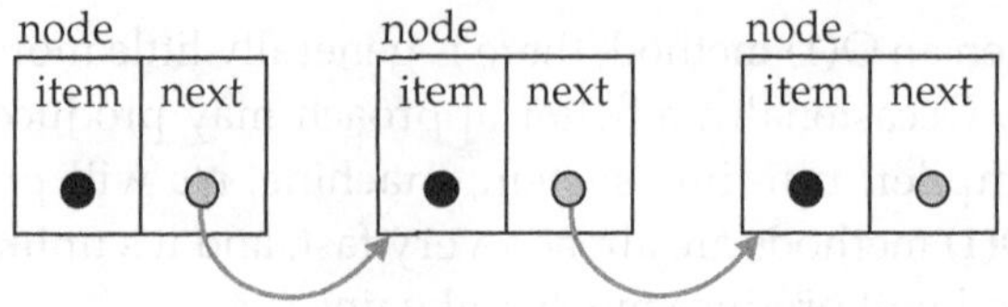

Each node of the list has two elements

1. the item being stored in the list and
2. a pointer to the next item in the list The last node in the list contains a NULL pointer to indicate that it is the end or tail of the list.

As items are added to a list, memory for a node is dynamically allocated. Thus the number of items that may be added to a list is limited only by the amount of memory available. The variable (or handle) which represents the list is simply a pointer to the node at the head of the list.

Adding to a List

The simplest strategy for adding an item to a list is to:

(*a*) allocate space for a new node,

(*b*) copy the item into it,

(*c*) make the new node's next pointer point to the current head of the list and

(*d*) make the head of the list point to the newly allocated node.

3.9 LIST VARIANTS

3.9.1 Circularly Linked Lists

By ensuring that the tail of the list is always pointing to the head, we can build a circularly linked list. If the external pointer, points to the current "tail" of the list, then the "head" is found trivially via tail->next, permitting us to have either LIFO or FIFO lists with only one external pointer. In modern processors, the few bytes of memory saved in this way would probably not be regarded as significant. A circularly linked list would more likely be used in an application which required "round-robin" scheduling or processing.

3.9.2 Doubly Linked Lists

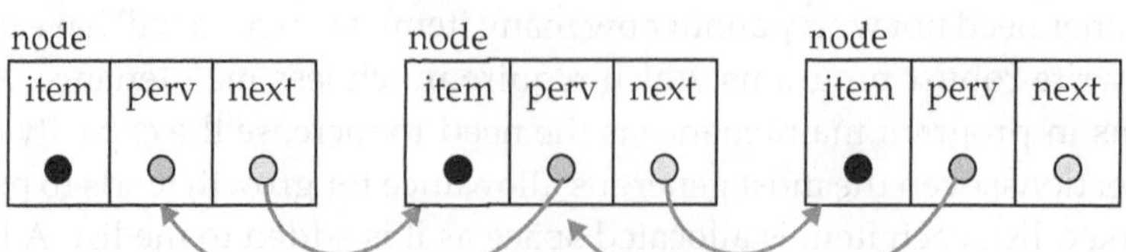

Doubly linked lists have a pointer to the preceding item as well as one to the next. They permit scanning or searching of the list in both directions. (To go backwards in a simple list, it is necessary to go back to the start and scan forwards.) Many applications require searching backwards and forwards through sections of a list: for example, searching for a common name like "Kim" in a Korean telephone directory would probably need much scanning backwards and forwards through a small region of the whole list, so the backward links become very useful. In this case, the node structure is altered to have two links:

```
struct t_node
  {
      void *item;
      struct t_node *previous;
      struct t_node *next;
  } node;
```

3.10 TREE

In computer science, a **tree** is a widely-used data structure that emulates a hierarchical tree structure with a set of linked nodes. It is an acyclic connected graph where each node has a set of zero or more *children* nodes, and at most one parent node.

3.10.1 Terminology

A node is a structure which may contain a value, a condition, or represent a separate data structure (which could be a tree of its own). Each node in a tree has zero or more **child nodes**, which are below it in the tree (by convention, trees grow down, not up as they do in nature). A node that has a child is called the child's **parent node** (or *ancestor node,* or superior). A node has at most one parent. Nodes at the bottommost level of the tree are called **leaf nodes**. Since they are at the bottommost level, they do not have any children. They are also referred to as **terminal nodes. The height** of a node is the length of the longest downward path to a leaf from that node. The height of the root is the height of the tree. The **depth** of a node is the length of the path to its root (*i.e.*, its *root path*). This is commonly needed in the manipulation of the various self balancing trees, AVL Trees in particular. Conventionally, the value-1 corresponds to a subtree with no nodes, whereas zero corresponds to a subtree with one node.The topmost node in a tree is called the **root node**. Being the topmost node, the root node will not have parents. It is the node at which operations on the tree commonly begin (although some algorithms begin with the leaf nodes and work up ending at the root). All other nodes can be reached from it by following **edges** or **links**. (In the formal definition, each such path is also unique). In diagrams, it is typically drawn at the top. In some trees, such as heaps, the root node has special properties. Every node in a tree can be seen as the root node of the subtree rooted at that node. An **internal node** or **inner node** is any node of a tree that has child nodes and is thus not a leaf node. A **subtree** of a tree T is a tree comprised of a node in T and all of its descendants in T. (This is different than the formal definition of subtree used in graph theory.)

The subtree corresponding to the root node is the entire tree; the subtree corresponding to any other node is called is a **proper subtree** (in analogy to the term proper subset).

3.10.2 Tree Representations

There are many different ways to represent trees; common representations represent the nodes as records allocated on the heap with pointers to their children, their parents, or both, or as items in an array, with relationships between them determined by their positions in the array (*e.g.*, binary heap).

3.10.3 Trees as Graphs

In graph theory, a tree is a connected acyclic graph. A rooted tree is such a graph with a vertex singled out as the root. In this case, any two vertices connected by an edge inherit a parent-child relationship. An acyclic graph with multiple connected components or a set of rooted trees is sometimes called a **forest**.

3.10.4 Traversal Methods

Stepping through the items of a tree, by means of the connections between parents and children, is called **walking the tree**, and the action is a **walk** of the tree. Often, an operation might be performed when a pointer arrives at a particular node. A walk in which each parent node is traversed before its children is called a **pre-order walk**; a walk in which the children are traversed before their respective parents are traversed is called a **post-order walk**.

3.10.5 Common Operations

1. Enumerating all the items
2. Enumerating a section of a tree
3. Searching for an item
4. Adding a new item at a certain position on the tree
5. Deleting an item
6. Removing a whole section of a tree (called pruning)
7. Adding a whole section to a tree (called grafting)
8. Finding the root for any node.

3.10.6 Common Uses

1. Manipulate hierarchical data
2. Make information easy to search
3. Manipulate sorted lists of data
4. As a workflow for compositing digital images for visual effects.

3.11 GRAPH

A graph is a finite set of nodes with edges between nodes. Formally, a graph G is a structure (V, E) consisting of a finite set V called the set of nodes, and a set E that is a subset of V. E is a set of pairs of the form (x,y) where x and y are nodes in V.

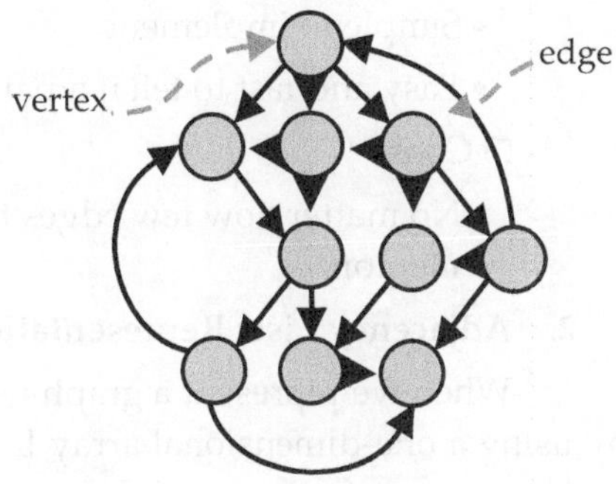

Fig. 3.6. Graph

A graph may be weighted and non-weighted. A **weighted graph** is one with weights (costs or lengths) on edges. If any graph is completely connected then it is known as complete Graph or Clique. We can define path in a particular graph, a **path** is a sequence of vertices connected by edges. Path of a graph sometime known as **cycle** if a path whose first and last vertices are the same and no vertex appears more than one time. The **in-degree** of a node x in G is the number of edges coming to x. The **out-degree** of x is the number of edges leaving x. A graph is **connected** if there is a path from any vertex to any other vertex otherwise disconnected.

3.11.1 Graph Representation

In computer science graph is very useful, they have to be conveniently represented in programs. In computer memory we can represent graph by using following two means.

1. Adjacency matrix representation
2. Adjacency lists representation

1. Adjacency Matrix Representation

When we represent a graph using adjacency matrix representation, each graph is represented by using matrix. Suppose if we want to represent a graph of N nodes then we need a matrix A of NXN that is, a two dimensional array. When we want to represent existence of any edge then we have to represent A $[i][j]$ = 1 (if I,j is an edge) otherwise A$[i][j]$ = 0(if I, j is not an edge).

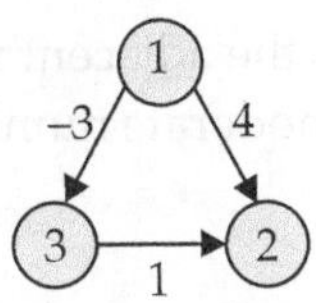

$$\begin{bmatrix} 0 & 1 & 1 \\ 0 & 0 & 0 \\ 0 & 1 & 0 \end{bmatrix}$$

	1	2	3
1	∞	4	–3
2	∞	∞	∞
3	∞	1	∞

Fig. 3.7. Representation of Graph Using Adjacency Matrix

Pros and Cons of Adjacency Matrices

❒ Pros:

- Simple to implement
- Easy and fast to tell if a pair (i,j) is an edge: simply check if A[i][j] is 1 or 0

❒ Cons:

- No matter how few edges the graph has, the matrix takes information for each edge in memory

2. **Adjacency Lists Representation**

When we represent a graph using adjacency list representation, each graph is represented by using a one-dimensional array L of linked lists where L[i] is the linked list containing all the nodes adjacent from node i. It is not compulsory that nodes in the list will follow any specific order.

For example, let's consider a graph consisting of vertices A, B and C, where the three vertices are in a triangular formation. Vertex A is adjacent to vertices B and C, vertex B is adjacent to vertices A and C, and finally, vertex C is adjacent to vertices A and B.

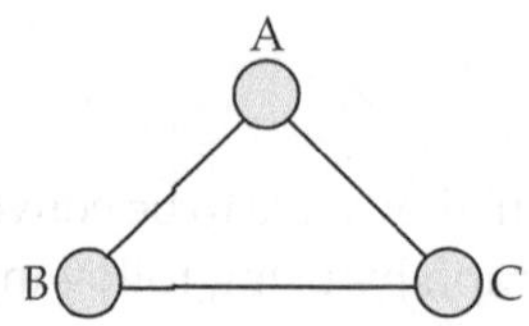

The resulting list would appear as follows:

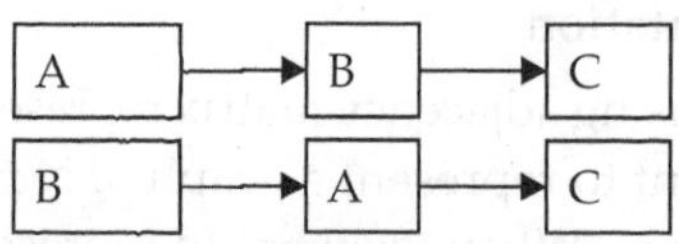

Fig. 3.8. Representation of Graph Using Adjacency List

The above adjacency list is easy to follow, and clearly illustrates the adjacent nature of the three vertices. It is most often used when the graph contains a small to moderate number of edges.

Pros and Cons of Adjacency Lists

❒ Pros:

- Saves on space (memory): the representation takes as many memory words as there are nodes and edge.

❒ Cons:

- It can take up to O(n) time to determine if a pair of nodes (i, j) is an edge: one would have to search the linked list L[i], which takes time proportional to the length of L[i].

3.11.2 Graph Traversal

Graphs, traversal means visiting every vertex in the graph only once (and you might process the value of that visited vertex). In sequential traversing of a list we start from the first element and finally reach the last element by sequentially incrementing the list's INDEX value by 1 every time, but if we are not following any sequential search pattern then we may start traversing from any vertex. (Tree traversal generally starts at root vertex.)

Two difficulties in graph traversal, but not in tree traversal:

- The graph may contain cycles;(we have to keep track of which vertices have been visited already)
- The graph may not be connected.

There are two important traversal methods:

- Breadth-first traversal, based on breadth-first search (BFS).
- Depth-first traversal, based on depth-first search (DFS).

Breadth-First Search

❒ DFS follows the following rules:

1. Select an unvisited node x, visit it, have it be the root in a BFS tree being formed. Its level is called the current level.
2. From each node z in the current level, in the order in which the level nodes were visited, visit all the unvisited neighbors of z. The newly visited nodes from this level form a new level that becomes the next current level.
3. Repeat step 2 until no more nodes can be visited.
4. If there are still unvisited nodes, repeat from Step 1.

Depth-First Search

❒ DFS follows the following rules:

1. Select an unvisited node x, visit it, and treat as the current node
2. Find an unvisited neighbor of the current node, visit it, and make it the new current node;
3. If the current node has no unvisited neighbors, backtrack to the its parent, and make that parent the new current node;
4. Repeat steps 3 and 4 until no more nodes can be visited.
5. If there are still unvisited nodes, repeat from step 1.

SUMMARY

We began by introducing the idea of a data structure as a way of organizing data in a computer's memory. We discussed how a computer's memory is organized as a long row of memory cells with each cell having a particular address. We also examined how these memory cells can contain the address of another memory cell. These pointers allow us to build very flexible and complex data structures. We examined a class of data structures called linear data structures that are organized in a linear fashion similar to the computer's memory. The first linear data structure was the ordered list. With this data structure we introduced the idea of abstraction and implementation. We saw there are two different ways to implement a list, but both implementations still have the same list operations. The second linear data structure was the stack. We discovered that the stack is really a list with the restriction that items can only be added and removed from the top of the stack. The third linear data structure was the queue. As we studied the queue, we found that our queue implementation had two distinct representations: logical and physical. In the logical representation, our queue was similar to a ring, but in the physical representation, our queue was actually implemented with an array. We looked at another class of data structures call non-linear data structures that are organized quite differently from the computer's memory. These data structures included multidimensional arrays, trees, and graphs. For each data structure, we examined one implementation of the data structure and discussed how the logical representation of the data structure was different from the physical representation. We introduced the idea of an abstract data type that groups a data structure with certain operations. These operations form an interface for the ADT through which the data structure can be manipulated.

EXERCISE

Stack operations

1. What would the state of a stack be after the following operations?

   Create stack

   Push A onto stack

   Push F onto stack

   Push X onto stack

   Pop item from stack

   Push B onto stack

   Pop item from stack

   Pop item from stack

2. Show the state of the stack and the value of each variable after execution of each of the following statements:

   A = 5 B = 3 C = 7

   (*a*) Create stack

   Push A onto stack

   Push C * C onto stack

   Pop item from stack and store in B

   Push B + A onto stack

   Pop item from stack and store in A

   Pop item from stack and store in B

   (*b*) Create stack

   Push B onto stack

   Push C onto stack

Push A onto stack
A = B ∗ C
Push A + C onto stack
Pop item from stack and store in A
Pop item from stack and store in B
Pop item from stack and store in C

3. Show how to implement a queue using two stacks. Analyze the running time of the queue operations.
4. Whereas a stack allows insertion and deletion of elements at only one end, and a queue allows insertion at one end and deletion at the other end, a ***deque*** (double-ended queue) allows insertion and deletion at both ends. Write four $O(1)$-time procedures to insert elements into and delete elements from both ends of a deque constructed from an array.

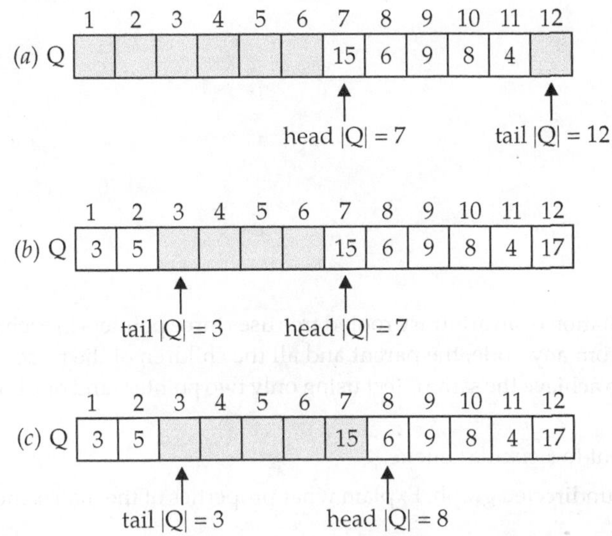

5. Using above figure as a model, illustrate the result of each of the operations ENQUEUE (Q,4),ENQUEUE(Q, 1), ENQUEUE(Q, 3), DEQUEUE(Q), ENQUEUE(Q, 8), and DEQUEUE(Q) on an initially empty queue Q stored in array Q [1.6].

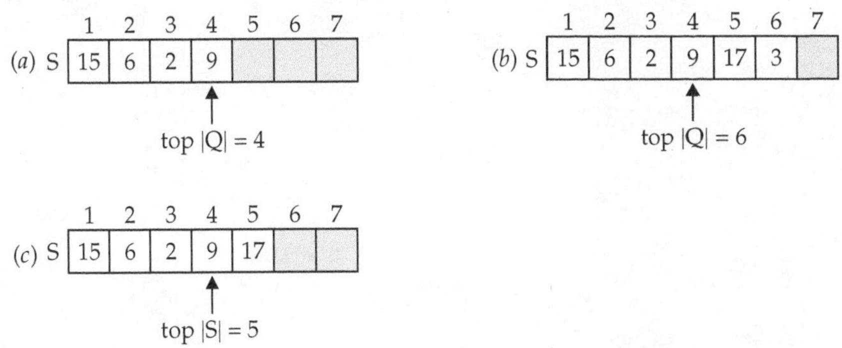

6. Using above figure as a model, illustrate the result of each of the operations PUSH(S, 4), PUSH(S, 1), PUSH(S, 3), POP(S), PUSH(S, 8), and POP(S) on an initially empty stack S stored in array S [1.6].

7. Explain how to implement doubly linked lists using only one pointer value *np*[*x*] per item instead of the usual two (*next* and *prev*). Assume that all index values can be interpreted as *k*-bit integers, and define *np*[*x*] to be *np*[*x*] = *next*[*x*] XOR *prev*[*x*], the *k*-bit "exclusive-or" of *next*[*x*] and *prev*[*x*]. (The value NIL is represented by 0.) Be sure to describe what information is needed to access the head of the list. Show how to implement the SEARCH, INSERT, and DELETE operations on such a list. Also show how to reverse such a list in O(1) time.
8. Implement a queue by a singly linked list L. The operations ENQUEUE and DEQUEUE should still take O(1) time.
9. Draw the binary tree rooted at index 6 that is represented by the following fields. *Index key left right*

   ....

   1. 12 7 3
   2. 15 8 NIL
   3. 4 10 NIL
   4. 10 5 9
   5. 2 NIL NIL
   6. 18 1 4
   7. 7 NIL NIL
   8. 14 6 2
   9. 21 NIL NIL
   10. 5 NIL NIL
10. The left-child, right-sibling representation of an arbitrary rooted tree uses three pointers in each node: *left-child, right-sibling*, and *parent*. From any node, the parent and all the children of the node can be reached and identified. Show how to achieve the same effect using only two pointers and one boolean value in each node.
11. Write an algorithm to add an element to a circular queue.
12. Let A be the adjacency matrix of an undirected graph. Explain what properties of the matrix indicate that:

    (*i*) The graph is complete

    (*ii*) The graph has a loop

    (*iii*) The graph has an isolated vertex.

Chapter 4 DIVIDE AND CONQUER STRATEGY

4.1 INTRODUCTION

In computer science, **divide and conquer** (D&C) is an important algorithm design paradigm. It works by recursively breaking down a problem into two or more sub-problems of the same (or related) type, until these become simple enough to be solved directly. The solutions to the sub-problems are then combined to give a solution to the original problem. This technique is the basis of efficient algorithms for all kinds of problems, such as sorting (quick sort, merge sort) and Fourier transform (FFT). The Divide and Conquer strategy can be viewed as one which has three steps. The first step is called **Divide** which is nothing but dividing the given problems into smaller sub-problems which are identical to the original problem and also these sub problems are of the same size. The second step is called **Conquer** wherein we solve these sub-problems recursively. The third step is called **Combine** wherein we combine the solutions of the sub-problems to get the solution for the original problem.

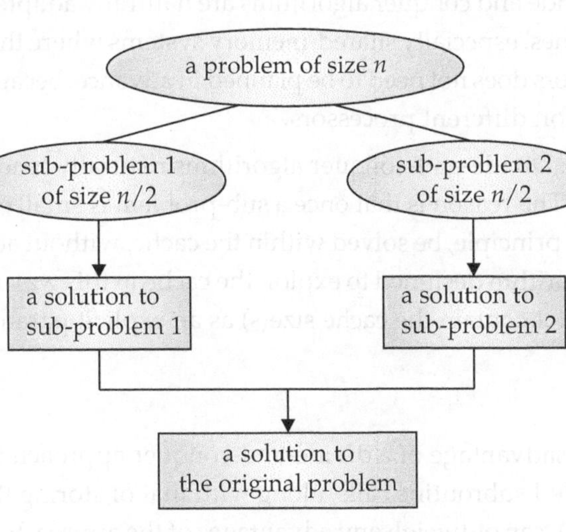

Fig. 4.1. Divide and Conquer Strategy

4.2 IMPLEMENTATION

Divide-and-conquer algorithms are naturally implemented as recursive procedures. In that case, the partial sub-problems leading to the one currently being solved implicitly stored in the procedure call stack. However, Divide and Conquer solutions can also be implemented by a non-recursive algorithm that stores the partial sub-problems in some explicit data structure, such as a stack, queue, or priority queue. This approach allows more freedom in the choice of the sub-problem that is to be solved next, a feature that is important in some applications *e.g.*, in breadth-first recursion and the branch and bound method for functions optimization.

Advantages

- **Solving difficult problems:** Divide and conquer is a powerful tool for solving conceptually difficult problems, such as the classic Tower of Hanoi puzzle: all it requires is a way of breaking the problem into sub-problems, and of solving the trivial cases. Indeed, for many such problems the paradigm offers the *only* simple solution.
- **Algorithm Efficiency:** Moreover, divide and conquer often provides a natural way to design efficient algorithms. For example, if the work of splitting the problem and combining the partial solutions is proportional to the problem's size n, there are a bounded number p of sub-problems of size $\sim n/p$ at each stage, and the base cases require O(1) (constant-bounded) time, then the divide-and-conquer algorithm will have $O(n \log n)$ complexity. This is used for problem such as sorting to reduce the complexity from $O(n^2)$, although in general there may also be other approaches to designing efficient algorithms.
- **Parallelism:** Divide and conquer algorithms are naturally adapted for execution in multi-processor machines, especially shared-memory systems where the communication of data between processors does not need to be planned in advance, because distinct sub-problems can be executed on different processors.
- **Memory Access:** Divide-and-conquer algorithms naturally tend to make efficient use of memory caches. The reason is that once a sub-problem is small enough, it and all its sub-problems can, in principle, be solved within the cache, without accessing the slower main memory. An algorithm designed to exploit the cache in this way is called cache oblivious, because it does not contain the cache size(s) as an explicit parameter.

Disadvantages

One commonly argued disadvantage of a divide-and-conquer approach is that recursion is slow: the overhead of the repeated subroutine calls, along with that of storing the call stack (the state at each point in the recursion), can outweigh any advantages of the approach. This, however, depends upon the implementation style: with large enough recursive base cases, the overhead of recursion can become negligible for many problems.

Another problem of a divide-and-conquer approach is that, for simple problems, it may be more complicated than a iterative approach, especially if large base cases are to be implemented for performance reasons. For example, to add N numbers, a simple loop to add them up in sequence is much easier to code than a divide-and-conquer approach that breaks the set of numbers into two halves, adds them recursively, and then adds the sums. (On the other hand, the latter approach turns out to be much more accurate in finite-precision floating-point arithmetic.)

Alternatively, an algorithm can be designed by a divide-and-conquer approach and then implemented in an iterative style; of course, any recursive algorithm can be simulated in an iterative style, but by reordering the computation it is sometimes possible to avoid simulating a recursive call stack altogether. The Cooley-Turkey FFT algorithm is a prime example of this: it was initially derived in a divide-and-conquer style, but implementations were traditionally implemented iteratively in a re-ordered fashion that avoided call-stack-like storage (although some recent implementations have returned to a recursive style).

Algorithm for divide and conquer

```
Algorithm D-and-C(n: input size)
if n≤n0      /* n0=small size problem*/
      Solve problem without futher sub-division;
else
      Divide into m sub-problems;
      Conquer the sub-problems by solving them
      independently and recursively;
      /* D-and-C(n/k) */
Combine the solutions;
```

4.3 APPLICATION OF DIVIDE AND CONQUER

4.3.1 Merge Sort

The problem considered here is to sort an array a of n comparable elements ($a[0], \ldots, a[n-1]$) to be non-decreasing. Let's look at how the divide-and-conquer steps are performed in merge sort algorithm. **Divide**-Split the elements to sort into two equal halves. To avoid copying portions of the array, typically the portion of the array being sorted is marked using a start index p and an end index r. The portion of the array being considered is $a[p] \ldots a[r]$. So for the initial problem $p = 0$ and $r = n - 1$. Let $q = b(p + r)/2c$. Then the problem of sorting $a[p] \ldots a[r]$ is divided into two sub-problems: sort $a[p] \ldots a[q]$ and sort $a[q + 1], \ldots, a[r]$. **Conquer** if either sub-array to sort has size 1 then just return. Otherwise, recursively sort the sub-array. **Combine**-Merge the two sorted sub-arrays. An important component of this algorithm is that merging two sorted sub-arrays is asymptotically more efficient than sorting the original array. In particular, there is a simple linear time algorithm to merge two sorted arrays. A supplemental array is used to hold the sorted array, which can then be moved back into $a[p] \ldots a[r]$. An index of the current location (initially p) for the left half is maintained, an index of the current location (initially $q + 1$) of the right half is maintained, and an index of the current location into the supplemental array is maintained. Then the elements at the current locations of the left and right halves are compared. The smaller of these elements (or either if equal) are moved into the next open location in the supplemental array. Then the index of the array from which the element was moved is incremented and the index into the supplemental array is implemented. Since constant time is used at each step, and there is one step for each of the elements in the portion of a being sorted, this merge algorithm has linear worst-case asymptotic time complexity. For any given problem there can be more than one divide-and-conquer algorithm.

Algorithm for merge sort

```
MERGE-SORT(A, p, r)
{
    if (p == r) /* small size */
        return;
    else
        q=(p+r)/2;
        Merge-Sort(A, p, q);
        Merge-Sort(A, q + 1, r);
        Merge(A, p, q, r);
    }
    To sort the whole array, Merge-Sort(A, 1, n) is called
```

Complexity of merge sort

$$T(n) = \begin{cases} 2T(n/2) + O(n) & \text{if } n > 1 \\ n & \text{if } n = 1 \end{cases}$$

whose solution is $T(n) = O(n \log n)$.

Example:

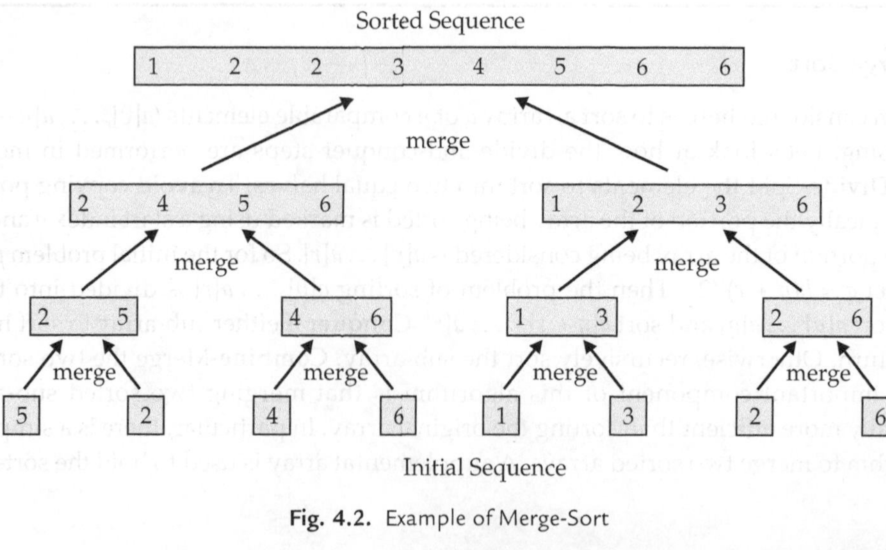

Fig. 4.2. Example of Merge-Sort

4.3.2 Quick-Sort

Quick-sort is an efficient and until lately fashionable sorting algorithm invented by C.A.R. Hoare in 1962. The Quick-sort algorithm requires $\Omega(\log n)$ extra storage space, making it not a strictly in-place algorithm. It is important to understand that **Quick-sort can go quadratic in the worst case.** The worst case time for Quick-sort is the same as for insertion sort and other simple algorithms, which is substantially worst than Heap-sort or Merge-sort.

The **partition phase** (in which the array is divided into two sub-arrays(partitions): **upper** that has values less then pivot and **lower** which has values greater or equal then pivot. This process is then repeated recursively on each partition.

The **sort phase** which is performed when the partition became reasonably small, say 5 elements. The sort phase use some simple sort algorithm (for example selection sort) to sort each small partition which are generated in the partition phase. This phase is optional as the first phase can run till the partitions of size 1. In pseudo-code the algorithm looks like:

- Pick one element in the array, which will be the *pivot*.
- Make one pass through the array, called a *partition* step, re-arranging the entries so that: the pivot is in its proper place.
- Entries smaller than the pivot are to the left of the pivot.
- Entries larger than the pivot are to its right.
- Recursively apply Quick-sort to the part of the array that is to the left of the pivot, and to the part on its right until the size of the partition is less than predefined small number M. For example, M = 5. Then apply some simple sorting algorithm to each partition. If M = 1 then sorting phase is not needed. It is clear that the main work is done in the partition phase so the quality of division of two sub-partitions is crucial. For the strategy to be effective, the partition phase must ensure that two partitions are almost equal in size. This is pretty complex problem that actually does not have satisfactory solutions. The most common solution is "selection-based pivoting" In worst case one of the partitions is of size one and Quick-sort becomes very inefficient. Also problematic are:

1. Reversely sorted arrays, where a lot of useless work is done on each partition moving elements.
2. Arrays with a few distinct elements (high number of occurrences of the same number).
3. Nearly sorted arrays (algorithms is being to pre-existing sorting order).

As you can see we choose a *pivot* element and arrange that all the items in the lower part are less than the pivot and all those in the upper part greater than it. In the most general case, we don't know anything about the items to be sorted, so that any choice of the pivot element will do-the first element is a convenient one.

Algorithm for Quick Sort

```
QUICK-SORT(A, p, r)
if (p==r)/* small size problem*/
return;
else
q:=Partition(A, p, r);
Quick-Sort(A, p, q-1);
Quick-Sort(A, q+1, r);
To sort the whole array, Quick-Sort(A, 1, n) is called.
```

$$T(n) = \begin{cases} 2T(n/2) + O(n) & \text{if } n > 1 \\ 0 & \text{if } n = 1 \end{cases}$$

Whose solution is $T(n) = O(n \log n)$. The worst case time complexity of the algorithm is $O(n^2)$.

Example:

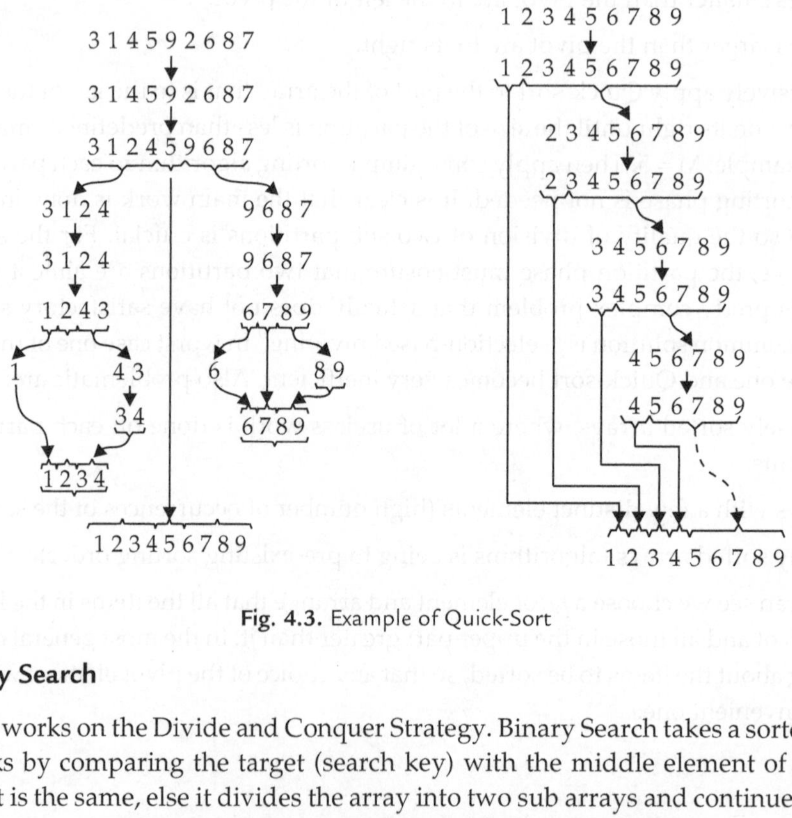

Fig. 4.3. Example of Quick-Sort

4.3.3 Binary Search

Binary Search works on the Divide and Conquer Strategy. Binary Search takes a sorted array as the input. It works by comparing the target (search key) with the middle element of the array and terminates if it is the same, else it divides the array into two sub arrays and continues the search in left (right) sub array if the target is less (greater) than the middle element of the array. Reducing the problem size by half is part of the **Divide** step in Binary Search and searching in this reduced problem space is part of the **Conquer** step in Binary Search. There is no **Combine** step in Binary Search.

Binary Search algorithm

```
1. Begin
2. Set left = 1, right = n
3. While (left ≤ right) do
     3.1 m = middle ((left + right)/2)
     3.2 If (target = a[m]) then End with output as m
     3.3 If (target < a[m]) then right = m - 1
     3.4 If (target > a[m]) then left = m +1
4. End with output as none
The basic operation here is comparison.
```

Worst Case Analysis: Step 3.2 to Step 3.4 each performs 1 comparison and these steps executes **logn** times. **logn** is the number of times the while loop executes. Each time we are reducing the problem size by half. *i.e.* $n/2$, $n/4$, $n/8$, ... The loop terminates when we hit on a single element array and this would occur when the while loop has executed **logn** times. The maximum number of comparisons in Binary Search would be **3 * logn**. Hence the worst case complexity of Binary search is **O(logn)**.

Running time = time to divide the array into two sub arrays + one checking

$$T(n) = T(n / 2) + 1,$$

where $T(1) = 1$

$$T(n / 2) = T(n / 4) + 1$$

....

$$T(4) = T(2) + 1$$

$$T(2) = T(1) + 1 = \mathbf{\log 2 + 1}$$

Backtracking,

$$T(4) = 2 + 1 = \log 4 + 1$$

$$T(n) = \log n + 1$$

$$T(n) = O(\log n)$$

This binary search is more efficient than linear search but needs the elements in a sorted manner.

Example Binary Search to seek element 123

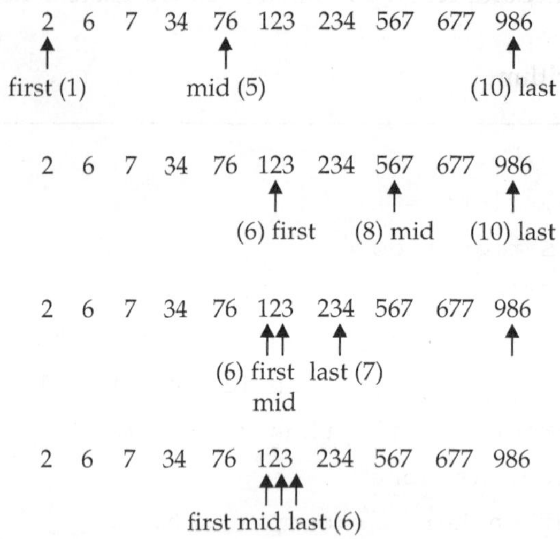

Fig. 4.4. Example Binary Search

4.3.4 Strassen's Matrix Multiplication

The standard method of matrix multiplication of two $n \times n$ matrices takes $O(n^3)$ operations. Strassen's algorithm is a Divide-and-Conquer algorithm that is asymptotically faster, *i.e.*, $O(nlg)$. The usual multiplication of two 2×2 matrices takes 8 multiplications and 4 additions. Strassen showed how two 2×2 matrices can be multiplied using only 7 multiplications and 18 additions. For 2×2 matrices, there is no benefit in using the method. To see where this is of help, think about multiplication two $(2k) \times (2k)$ matrices. For this problem, the scalar multiplications and additions become matrix multiplications and additions. An addition of two matrices requires $O(k^2)$ time, a multiplication requires $O(k^3)$. • Hence, multiplications are much more expensive and it makes sense to trade one multiplication operation for 18 additions. Imagine that A and B are each partitioned into four square sub-matrices, each sub-matrix having dimensions $n \times n$. then we can solve $2k \times 2k$ matrices faster and conveniently using strassen's.

$$\begin{pmatrix} A_{11} & A_{12} \\ A_{21} & A_{22} \end{pmatrix} \times \begin{pmatrix} B_{11} & B_{12} \\ B_{21} & B_{22} \end{pmatrix} = \begin{pmatrix} C_{11} & C_{12} \\ C_{21} & C_{22} \end{pmatrix}$$

Multiplication by classical method:

$$C_{11} = A_{11}B_{11} + A_{12}B_{21}$$

$$C_{12} = A_{11}B_{12} + A_{12}B_{22}$$

$$C_{21} = A_{21}B_{11} + A_{22}B_{21}$$

$$C_{22} = A_{21}B_{12} + A_{22}B_{22}$$

Algorithm for classical matrix multiplication:

```
Void matrix_mult()
{
  for (i=1;i<=n;i++)
      for (j=1;j<=n;j++)
  compute C_ij;
  }
  }
  }
```

$$C_{i,j} = \sum_{k=1}^{N} a_{i,k}\, b_{k,j}$$

Thus $$TN = \sum_{i=1}^{N} \sum_{j=1}^{N} \sum_{k=1}^{N} c = cN^3 = O(N^3)$$

But Strassen "observed" that:

$$\begin{pmatrix} C_{11} & C_{12} \\ C_{21} & C_{22} \end{pmatrix} = \begin{pmatrix} P_5 + P_4 - P_2 + P_6 & P_1 + P_2 \\ P_3 + P_4 & P_5 + P_1 - P_3 - P_7 \end{pmatrix}$$

where,

$$P_1 = A_{11}(B_{12} - B_{22})$$
$$P_2 = (A_{11} + A_{12})B_{22}$$
$$P_3 = (A_{21} + A_{22})B_{11}$$
$$P_4 = A_{22}(B_{21} - B_{11})$$
$$P_5 = (A_{11} + A_{22})(B_{11} + B_{22})$$
$$P_6 = (A_{12} - A_{22})(B_{21} + B_{22})$$
$$P_7 = (A_{11} - A_{21})(B_{11} + B_{12})$$

Strassen showed that 2 × 2 matrix multiplication can be accomplished in 7 multiplication and 18 additions or subtractions. This reduce can be done by Divide and Conquer Approach.

Algorithm for Strassen's Matrix Multiplication:

```
Void matmul(int *A, int *B, int *R, int n) {
  if (n == 1) {
     (*R) += (*A) * (*B);
  } else {
matmul(A, B, R, n/4);
```

```
matmul(A, B+(n/4)+ R+(n/4), n/4);
matmul(A+2*(n/4), B, R+2*(n/4), n/4);
    matmul(A+2*(n/4), B+(n/4), R+3*(n/4), n/4);
    matmul(A+(n/4), B+2*(n/4), R, n/4);
    matmul(A+(n/4), B+3*(n/4), R+(n/4), n/4);
    matmul(A+3*(n/4), B+2*(n/4), R+2*(n/4), n/4);
    matmul(A+3*(n/4), B+3*(n/4), R+3*(n/4), n/4);
}
```

Complexity Calculation for strassen's matrix multiplication:

```
T(1)=1  {Assume N=2^k}
T(N)=7T(N/2)
T(N)=7^k T(N/2^k)=7^k
T(N)=7^logN=N^log7=N^2.81
```

$T(n) = 7T(n^2) + cn^2$, where c is a fixed constant. The term cn^2 captures the time for the matrix additions and subtractions needed to compute $P_1, ..., P_7$ and $C_{11}, ..., C_{22}$.

The solution works out to be:

$$\mathbf{T(n) = \theta (n^{lg7}) = O(n^{2.81}).}$$

Currently, the best known algorithm was given by Coppersmith and Winograd and has time complexity

$$O(n^{2.376}).$$

Example of Strassen's

$$\begin{pmatrix} 7 & 9 \\ 2 & 5 \end{pmatrix} \times \begin{pmatrix} 3 & 2 \\ 6 & 5 \end{pmatrix}$$

$$\begin{aligned} P_1 &= A_{11}(B_{12} - B_{22}) \\ &= 7(2-5) \\ &= -21 \\ P_2 &= (A_{11} + A_{12})\, B_{22} \\ &= (7+9)5 \\ &= 80 \\ P_3 &= (A_{21} + A_{22})\, B_{11} \\ &= (2+5)3 \\ &= 21 \end{aligned}$$

$$
\begin{aligned}
P_4 &= A_{22}\,(B_{21}\ \ B_{11}) \\
&= 5(6 - 3) \\
&= 15 \\
P_5 &= (A_{11} + A_{22})\,(B_{11} + B_{22}) \\
&= (7 + 5)(3 + 5) \\
&= 12 * 8 \\
&= 96 \\
P_6 &= (A_{12} - A_{22})\,(B_{21} + B_{22}) \\
&= (9 - 5)(6 + 5) \\
&= 4 * 11 \\
&= 44 \\
P_7 &= (A_{21} - A_{11})\,(B_{11} + B_{12}) \\
&= (7 - 2)(3 + 2) \\
&= 25 \\
C_{11} &= P_5 + P_4 - P_2 + P_6 \\
&= 96 + 15 - 80 + 44 \\
&= 75 \\
C_{12} &= P_1 + P_2 \\
&= -21 + 80 \\
&= 59 \\
C_{21} &= P_3 + P_4 \\
&= 21 + 15 \\
&= 36 \\
C_{22} &= P_5 + P_1 - P_3 - P_7 \\
&= 96 + (-21) - 21 - 25 \\
&= 29
\end{aligned}
$$

4.4 RECURRENCE RELATION

Definition: Recurrence relations are recursive definitions of mathematical functions or sequences. A recurrence relation express the running time of recursive algorithm. This includes how many recursive calls are generated at each level of the recursion, how much of the problem is solved by each recursive call, and how much work is done at each level. A recurrence is an equation or inequalitity that describes a function in terms of its value on smaller inputs. To solve a recurrence relat ion means to obtain a function defined on the natural numbers that satisfies the recurrence.

For example, the recurrence relation of MERGE-SORT

$$T(n) = \begin{cases} \Theta(1) & \text{if } n = 1 \\ 2T(n/2) + \Theta(n) & \text{if } n > 1 \end{cases}$$

4.4.1 Methods to Solve Recurrence Relations

(1) Substitution Method

(2) Iteration Method

(3) Master Method

1. **Substitution Method:** In the substitution method we guess a bound and then use mathematical induction to prove our guess correct. This is a good method for solving recurrence relation,but it can be applied only in case when it is easy to guess the form of the answer. The substitution method can be used to establish either upper or lower bounds on a recurrence.

Example 1: *Consider the recurrence T(n) = 2T([n/2] + 16) + n we have to show that it is asymptotically bound by O(nlogn).*

Solution: For T(n) = O(nlog n) we have to show that some constant c such that T(n) < = cnlog n.

Put this in given recurrence equation.

$$\begin{aligned} T(n) &<= 2[c([n/2] + 16) \log([n/2] + 16)] + n \\ &= cn\log(n/2) + 32 + n \\ &= cn\log n - cn\log 2 + 32 + n \\ &= cn\log n - cn + 32 + n \\ &= cn\log n - (c-1)\,n + 32 \\ &<= cn\log n (\text{for } c >= 1) \end{aligned}$$

Thus $T(n) = O(n\log n)$

Example 2: *Consider the recurrence T(n) = T([n/2] + 1 we have to show that it is asymptotically bound by O(logn).*

For T(n) = O(log n) we have to show that some constant c such that T(n) <= clogn.

Solution:

Put this in given recurrence equation.

$$\begin{aligned} T(n) &<= c\log([n/2]) + 1 \\ &= c\log(n/2)+1 \\ &= c\log n - c\log 2 + 1 \\ &<= c\log n \ (\text{for } c > = 1) \end{aligned}$$

Thus $T(n) = O(\log n)$

Example 3: *Consider the recurrence T(n) = 2T([n/2] + n we have to show that it is asymptotically bound by O(nlog n).*

Solution: For T(n) = O(n log n) we have to show that some constant c such that T(n) <= c nlog n.

Put this in given recurrence equation.

$$T(n) <= 2c\,[n/2] \log ([n/2]) + n$$
$$= cn \log n - cn \log 2 + n$$
$$= c \log n - n(c \log 2 - 1)$$
$$<= cn \log n \text{ (for } c >= 1)$$

Thus $T(n) = O(n \log n)$

2. **Iteration Method:** This method converts the recurrence into a summation and then relies on techniques for bounding summation to solve the recurrence. The basic idea behind iteration method is to expand the recurrence and express it as a summation of terms dependent only on 'n' and the initial condition.

Example 4: *Consider the recurrence $T(n) = 2T([n/3]) + n$ we have to show that it is asymptotically bound by $O(n)$.*

Solution: $T(n) = 2T([n/3]) + n$

Expanding the above terms,

$$T(n) = n + 2/3n + 4T(n/9)$$
$$= n + 2/3n + 4/9n + 8T(n/27)$$

It is to be noticed that we can meet boundary condition where $(n/3^i) <= 1$, *i.e.,* after performing $[\log 3n]$ expansions. Thus,

$$T(n) = O(n).$$

Example 5: *Consider the recurrence $T(n) = T(n-1) + 1$ and $T(1) = \theta(1)$ Solve it.*

Solution: $T(n) = T(n-1) + 1$

$$= (T(n-2) + 1) + 1$$
$$= (T(n-3) + 1) + 1 + 1$$
$$= T(n-4) + 4$$
$$= T(n-5) + 5$$
$$= T(n-k) + k$$

where $k = n - 1$

i.e., $T(n-k) = T(1) = \theta(1)$

i.e., $T(n) = \theta(1) + (n-1) = 1 + n - 1 = n = \theta(n)$

3. **Master Method:** Let $T(n)$ be defined on non-negative integers by the recurrence.
$T(n) = aT(n/b) + f(n)$ where $a = 1$ and $b > 1$ be constant anf $f(n)$ be a function.
Then $T(n)$ can be bound asymptotically as follows:
   1. If $f(n) = O(n \log_b a - \varepsilon)$ for some constant $\varepsilon > 0$, then $T(n) = \theta(n\log_b{}^a)$
   2. If $f(n) = \theta(n \log_b{}^a)$ then $T(n) = \theta(n \log_b{}^a \log n)$
   3. If $f(n) = \Omega(n \log_b{}^{a+\varepsilon})$ for some constant $\varepsilon > 0$ and if $f(n/b) <= c f(n)$ for some $c < 1$ and all sufficiently large n, then $T(n) = \theta(f(n))$, $f(n/b) <= cf(n)$ is called the **regularity** condition.

Example 6: *Solve the recurrence using master method.*

$$T(n) = 9T(n/3) + n$$

Solution: Compare the given recurrence with **T(n) = aT(n/b) + f(n).**

We get, $a = 9, b = 3\ f(n) = n$

Now, $n^{\log_b a} = n^{\log_3 9} = n^2 = \theta(n^2)$

By using condition 1 we get,

$$f(n) = n = n^{\log_3 9-1} = n^{2-1}$$

Hence the solution is $T(n) = \theta(n^{\log_b a}) = \theta(n^{\log_3 9}) = \theta(n^2)$.

Example 7: *Solve the recurrence using master method.*

$$T(n) = T(2n/3) + 1$$

Solution: Compare the given recurrence with **T(n) = aT(n/b) + f(n).**

We get, $a = 1, b = 3/2\ f(n) = 1$

Now, $n^{\log_b a} = n^{\log_{3/2} 1} = n^0 = 1$

$$f(n) = n^{\log_b a},$$

Hence case 2 applies, Thus solution is

$$T(n) = \theta(n^{\log_b a} \log n) = \theta(\log n)$$

Example 8: *Solve the recurrence using master method.*

$$T(n) = 3T(n/4) + n \log n$$

Solution: Compare the given recurrence with **T(n) = aT(n/b) + f(n).**

We get, $a = 3, b = 4\ f(n) = n \log n$

Now, $n^{\log_b a} = n^{\log_4 3} = O(n^{0.793})$

$$f(n) = \Omega(n^{\log_4 3 + \varepsilon}) \text{ where } \varepsilon = 0.2$$

case 3 applies now for regularity condition *i.e.,*

$$af(n/b) <= cf(n)$$

$$3(n/4) \log(n/4) <= (3/4)\, n \log n = cf(n) \text{ for } c = 3/4$$

Therefore the solution is $T(n) = \theta(n \log n)$

Applications: Recurrence relations are a fundamental mathematical tool since they can be used to represent mathematical functions/sequences that cannot be easily represented non-recursively. An example is the Fibonacci sequence.

Analyzing (recursive) algorithms using recurrence relations: For recursive algorithms, it is convenient to use recurrence relations to describe the time complexity functions of the algorithms. Then, we can obtain the time complexity estimates by solving the recurrence relations. Here is an example. Given algorithm

Algorithm Test (A[1..*n*], B[1..*n*], C[1..*n*]);

```
if n=0 then return;
For i:=1 to n do
   C[1]:=A[1]*B[i];
call Test (A[2..n], B[2..n], C[2..n]);
```

If we denote the time complexity of Test as T(n), then we can express T(n) recursively as an recurrence relation:

$$T(n) = T(n-1) + O(n)$$
$$T(1) = 1$$

By a straightforward expansion method, we can solve T(n) as:

$$\begin{aligned} T(n) &= T(n-1) + O(n) \\ &= (T(n-2) + O(n-1)) + O(n) \\ &= T(n-2) + O(n-1) + O(n) \\ &= T(n-3) + O(n-2) + O(n-1) + O(n) \\ &\dots \\ &= T(1) + O(2) + \dots + O(n-1) + O(n) \\ &= O(1 + 2 + \dots + n - 1 + n) \\ &= O(n\wedge 2) \end{aligned}$$

Yet another example:

Algorithm Parallel-Product (A[1..n]);

```
if n=1 then return;
for i:=1 to n/2 do
   A[i]:=A[i]*A[i + n/2];
call Parallel-Product (A[1..n/2]);
```

The time complexity of the above algorithm can be expressed as

$$T(n) = T(n/2) + O(n/2)$$
$$T(1) = 1$$

We can solve it as:

$$\begin{aligned} T(n) &= T(n/2) + O(n/2) \\ &= (T(n/2\wedge 2) + O(n/2\wedge 2)) + O(n/2) \\ &= T(n/2\wedge 2) + O(n/2\wedge 2) + O(n/2) \\ &= T(n/2\wedge 3) + O(n/2\wedge 3) + O(n/2\wedge 2) + O(n/2) \\ &\dots \\ &= T(n/2\wedge i) + O(n/2\wedge i) + \dots + O(n/2\wedge 2) + O(n/2) \\ &= T(n/2\wedge \log n) + O(n/2\wedge \log n) + \dots + O(n/2\wedge 2) + O(n/2) \end{aligned}$$

// We stop the expansion at $i = \log n$ because $2\wedge \log n = n$ //

$$\begin{aligned} &= T(1) + O(n/2\wedge \log n) + \dots + O(n/2\wedge 2) + O(n/2) \\ &= 1 + O(n/2\wedge \log n + \dots + n/2\wedge 2 + n/2) \\ &= 1 + O(n*(1/2\wedge \log n + \dots + 1/2\wedge 2 + 1/2) \\ &= O(n) \end{aligned}$$

// because $1/2\wedge \log n + \dots + 1/2\wedge 2 + 1/2 <= 1$ //

Using recurrence relations to develop algorithms: Recurrence relations are useful in the design of algorithms, as in the dynamic programming paradigm. For this course, you only need to know how to derive an iterative (dynamic programming) algorithm when you are given a recurrence relation.

For example, given the recurrence relation for the Fibonacci function $f(n)$ above, we can convert it into DP algorithm as follows:

Algorithm Fib(n);

```
var f[0..n]: array of integers;
f[0]: = f[1]: = 1;
for i: = 2 to n do
   f[i]: = f[i - 1] + f[i - 2];
      //following the recurrence relation //
return f[n];
```

The time complexity of this algorithm is easily seen as O(n). Of course you may also easily derive a recursive algorithm from the recurrence relation:

Algorithm Fib-Rec(n);

```
if n=0 or 1 then return 1;
else
   return Fib-Rec(n - 1) + Fib-Rec(n - 2);
```

but the time complexity of this algorithm will be exponential, since we can write its time complexity function recursively as:

$$T(n) = T(n - 1) + T(n - 2)$$

$$T(1) = T(0) = 1$$

In other words, T(n) is exactly the nth Fibonacci number.

SUMMARY

In this chapter, we cover divide-and-conquer algorithm design paradigm. It is an especially important concept in computer science because solving problems with it can increase the overall efficiency, thus reducing complexity (sometimes from n^2 we can reduce it to n * log n). Additionally, its elegance should definitely be appreciated. Here are a few conclusions regarding D and C. It is generally advisable to analyze the complexity of a D and C algorithm to see whether or not you gain efficiency. Most of the time, they lead to really efficient algorithms which work great on large numbers and so forth, but you may complicate things when only a very small amount of data will be worked. There are lots of other examples of problems that are specifically suitable for solving with D and C; you can Google a few. These include such problems as Hanoi Tower, Koch Fractals, Karatsuba, Fibonacci Numbers, Matrix multiplication, Strassen's Algorithm.

EXERCISE

1. What is Divide and Conquer Strategy? Give it's pros and cons.
2. Consider following list of elements as 49, 39, 19, 69, 14, 34, 19, 59. Sort the above using merge sort.
3. Among merge sort and quick sort which technique is best in worst case? Justify your answer with an example.
4. Analyze merge sort algorithm for best case, worst case & average case.
5. What is the running time of quick-sort when all elements of array Quick have the same value ?
6. Show how quick sorts the following sequence of keys.

   (*a*) 1, 2, 17, 16, 4, 3

   (*b*) 3, 3, 3, 3, 3, 3, 3

   (*c*) 2, 2, 7, 9, 9, 5, 4, 4, 1

   (*d*) 1, 3, 5, 7, 9, 12, 15
7. Define Binary Search in brief.
8. Consider the recurrence T*n* = 3T*n* – 1 + 1, T0 = 0 Guess the solution , and prove it by induction.
9. Write the quick sort algorithm. Analyze its efficiency. Apply the algorithm to sort the list {4, 1, 6, 3, 9, 2, 7, 5}.
10. Explain the general plan for analyzing the efficiency of a recursive algorithm.
11. Solve the following recurrence relations.

    (*i*) $x(n) = x(n-1) + 5$ for $n > 1$, $x(1) = 0$

    (*ii*) $x(n) = 3x(n-1)$ for $n > 1$, $x(1) = 4$.
12. Solve the recurrence using master method.

    (*i*) $T(n) = 16T(n/4) + n^3$

    (*ii*) $T(n) = 2T(n/2) + n^3$

    (*iii*) $T(n) = 5T(n/4) + n^2$

    (*iv*) $T(n) = 7T(n/2) + n^2$

    (*v*) $T(n) = 2T(n/2) + n^2$.

Chapter 5 GREEDY METHOD

5.1 INTRODUCTION

Greedy method is a method of choosing a subset of the dataset as the solution set that result in some profit. Consider a problem having n inputs; we are required to obtain the solution which is a series of subsets that satisfy some constraints or conditions. Any subset, which satisfies these constraints, is called a feasible solution. It is required to obtain the feasible solution that maximizes or minimizes the objective function. This feasible solution finally obtained is called optimal solution. If one can devise an algorithm that works in stages, considering one input at a time and at each stage, a decision is taken on whether the data chosen results with an optimal solution or not. If the inclusion of a particular data results with an optimal solution, then the data is added into the partial solution set. On the other hand, if the inclusion of that data results with infeasible solution then the data is eliminated from the solution set.

In general, greedy algorithms have five pillars:

- A **candidate set**, from which a solution is created
- A **selection function**, which chooses the best candidate to be added to the solution
- A **feasibility function**, that is used to determine if a candidate can be used to contribute to a solution
- An **objective function**, which assigns a value to a solution, or a partial solution, and a solution function, which will indicate when we have discovered a complete solution.

Greedy algorithms produce good solutions on some mathematical problems, but not on others. Most problems for which they work well have two properties:

Greedy Choice Property

We can make whatever choice seems best at the moment and then solve the subproblems that arise later. The choice made by a greedy algorithm may depend on choices made so far but not on future choices or all the solutions to the subproblem. It iteratively makes one greedy choice after another, reducing each given problem into a smaller one. In other words, a greedy algorithm never reconsiders its choices. This is the main difference from dynamic programming, which is exhaustive and is guaranteed to find the solution. After every stage, dynamic programming makes decisions based on all the decisions made in the previous stage, and may reconsider the previous stage's algorithmic path to solution.

Optimal Substructure

"A problem exhibits optimal substructure if an optimal solution to the problem contains optimal solutions to the sub-problems." Said differently, a problem has optimal substructure if the best next move always leads to the optimal solution. An example of 'non-optimal substructure' would be a situation where capturing a queen in chess (good next move) will eventually lead to the loss of the game (bad overall move).

Greedy Algorithm

1. {*a*[1..*n*] is an array containing *n* inputs}
2. Solution <–Empty
3. For *i* <–1 to *n* do
4. X<–SELECT(*a*); [as per some optimization criteria]
5. If FEASIBLE (Solution, X) then
6. Solution<-UNION(Solution, X)
7. End
8. End
9. Return solution.

where,

SELECT(): Select an element from a[] such that it has a potential for satisfying the optamility criteria or selection policies.

FEASIBLE(): Feasible function checks if the selected element is *x* satisfies the feasibility criteria.

UNION(): Union function integrates the element in solution.

Example of Greedy choice property:

Problem: Pick *k* numbers out of *n* numbers such that the sum of these k number is largest.

```
Algorithm(Largest)
For i=1 to k
Pick out the largest number
Delete these numbers from input.
End for
```

Example: 9, 12, 15, 3, 7, 2, 1, 13, 8

- Pick four number which sum is largest
- Pick four number which sum is not greater than 15.

Some more examples

- Money to be return 2.89 and coins available:

1 ₹ 25 Paisa, 10 Paisa, 5 paisa, 1 Paisa you may use total 10 coins:

Solution: 2 coins = 1 ₹

3 coins = 25 paisa

1 coin = 10 paisa

4 coins = 1 paisa.

- Money to be return 5.96 and coins available:

200 Paisa, 100 Paisa, 50 Paisa, 20 Paisa, 5 Paisa, 2 paisa, 1 Paisa you may use total 8 coins solve it.

5.2 APPLICATIONS OF GREEDY METHOD

There are five types of greedy methods under as follows:

1. Activity Scheduling Problem
2. Container Loading Problem
3. Minimum Spanning Tree
4. Knapsack Problem
5. Single Source Shortest Path Problem

5.2.1 Activity Scheduling Problem

Definition: In a scheduling problem one has to find time slots in which activities (or jobs) should be processed under given constraints. The main constraints are resource constraints and precedence constraints between activities. A quite general scheduling problem is the Resource Constrained Project Scheduling Problem (RCPSP) which can be formulated as follows:

We have Activities $j = 1, \ldots, n$ with processing times p_j. Resources $k = 1, \ldots, r$. A constant amount of R_k units of resource k is available at any time. During processing, activity j occupies r_{jk} units of resource k for $k = 1, \ldots, r$. Precedence constrains $i \rightarrow j$ between some activities i, j with the meaning that activity j cannot start before i is finished..

The objective is to determine starting times S_j for all activities j in such a way that at each time t the total demand for resource k is not greater than the availability R_k for $k = 1, \ldots, r$, the given precedence constraints are fulfilled, *i.e.*, $S_i + p_i \leq S_j$ if $i \rightarrow j$, some objective function $f(C_1, \ldots, C_n)$ is minimized where $C_j = S_j + p_j$ is the completion time of activity j. The fact that activities j start at time S_j and finish at time $S_j + p_j$ implies that the activities j are not preempted. We may relax this condition by allowing preemption (activity splitting). If preemption is not allowed the vector S = (S_j) defines a schedule. S is called feasible if all resource and precedence constraints are fulfilled. One has to find a feasible schedule which minimizes the objective function $f(C_1, \ldots, C_n)$. In project planning $f(C_1, \ldots, C_n)$ is often replaced by the makespan C_{max} which is the maximum of all C_j -values.

Example:

Given: *Number of tasks, Start Time and End Time*

Task	*A*	*B*	*C*	*D*	*E*	*F*	*G*
Start Time	*0*	*3*	*4*	*9*	*7*	*1*	*6*
End Time	*2*	*7*	*7*	*11*	*10*	*5*	*8*

Solution: Arrange all the task on the basis of their start time in ascending order. Then plot a graph with maximum finish time. We can allot task A, B, E to machine m_1, F, G to machine m_2, and C, *d* to machine m_3.

5.2.2 Container Loading Problem

A large ship is loaded with the cargo. The cargo is containerized, and all container are of the same size. Different container may have different weight. The cargo capacity is C. We wish to load the ship with maximum number of container.

We have container $j = 1, \ldots, n$ with weight w_j. A cargo have the maximum capacity is C. Our aim is here to load the maximum container with constraint of capacity C.

Example 1: $N = 8$, $[w_1, w_2, w_3, w_4, w_5, w_6, w_7, w_8] = [100, 200, 50, 90, 150, 50, 20, 80]$ *and* $C = 400$ *Kg.*

Solution: We will arrange the containers in their increasing order according to weight. So, The sequence will be $[w_7, w_3, w_6, w_8, w_4, w_1, w_5, w_2]$ as we have the maximum capacity C = 400 Kg. So we can choose only following container $[w_7, w_3, w_6, w_8, w_4, w_1] = 390$ Kg.

Our solution will be, $[x_1, x_2, x_3, x_4, x_5, x_6, x_7, x_8] = [1, 0, 1, 1, 0, 1, 1, 1] = \Sigma xi = 6$

5.2.3 Minimum Spanning Tree

Definition: A spanning tree of a graph is just a sub-graph that contains all the vertices and its tree. A graph may have many spanning trees; for instance the complete graph on four vertices.

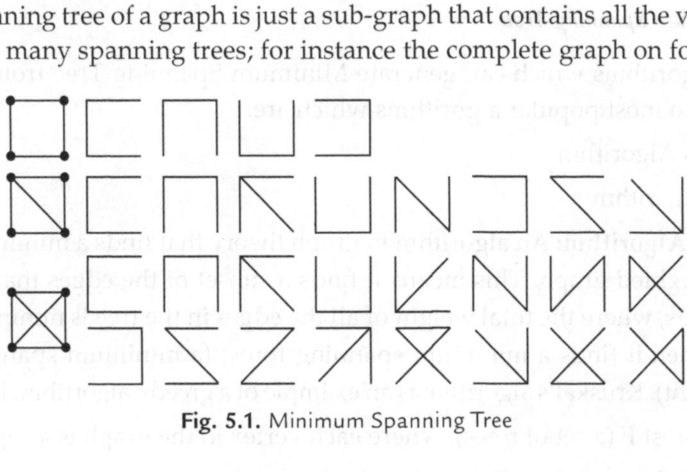

Fig. 5.1. Minimum Spanning Tree

Why Minimum Spanning Trees?

The standard application is to a problem like phone network design. You have a business with several offices; you want to lease phone lines to connect them up with each other; and the phone company charges different amounts of money to connect different pairs of cities. You want a set of lines that connects all your offices with a minimum total cost. It should be a spanning tree, since if a network isn't a tree you can always remove some edges and save money.

A less obvious application is that the minimum spanning tree can be used to approximately solve the traveling salesman problem. A convenient formal way of defining this problem is to find the shortest path that visits each point at least once.

Note that if you have a path visiting all points exactly once, it's a special kind of tree. In the example above, twelve of sixteen spanning trees are actually paths. If you have a path visiting some vertices more than once, you can always drop some edges to get a tree. So in general the MST weight is less than the TSP weight, because it's a minimization over a strictly larger set.

Application of Minimum Spanning Tree

- Construct a pipeline network to connect a number of towns using the smallest possible total length of the pipeline.
- Connecting terminals in cabling the panels of electrical equipment. How should we wire terminals to use the least possible length of the wire?
- Connecting different components of a digital computer system. Minimizing the length of wires reduces the capacitance and delay line effects.
- Connecting a number of computer sites by high-speed lines. Each line is leased and we want to minimize the leasing cost.
- All-pairs minimal path problem.

Algorithms for Minimum Spanning Tree

There are many algorithms which can generate Minimum Spanning Tree from the given forest. We will see here two most popular algorithms which are:

1. Kruskal's Algorithm
2. Prim's Algorithm

1. Kruskal's Algorithm: An algorithm in graph theory that finds a minimum spanning tree for a connected weighted graph. This means it finds a subset of the edges that forms a tree that includes every vertex, where the total weight of all the edges in the tree is minimized. If the graph is not connected, then it finds a minimum spanning forest (a minimum spanning tree for each connected component). Kruskal's algorithm is an example of a greedy algorithm. It works as follows:

- create a forest F (a set of trees), where each vertex in the graph is a separate tree
- create a set S containing all the edges in the graph

- while S is nonempty
  - o remove an edge with minimum weight from S
  - o if that edge connects two different trees, then add it to the forest, combining two trees into a single tree (if it form cycle)
  - o otherwise discard that edge.

Example:

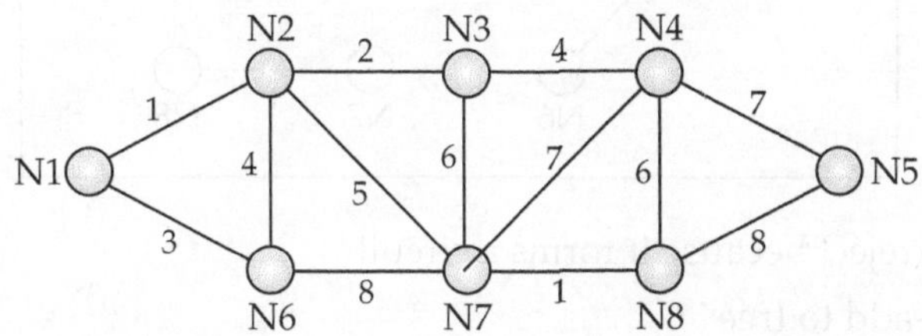

Using the above graph, here are the steps to the MST, using Kruskal's Algorithm with graphical representation:

N_1 to N_2-cost is 1-add to tree

Step 1:

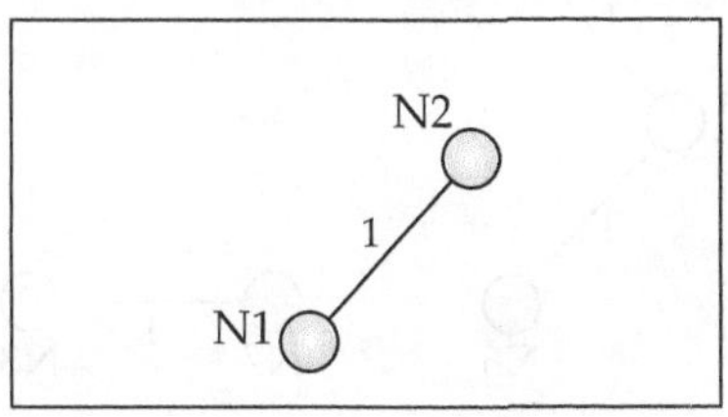

N_7 to N_8-cost is 1-add to tree

Step 2:

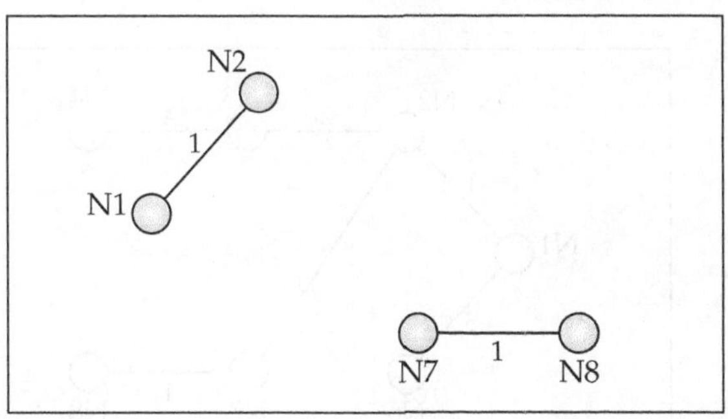

N_2 to N_3-cost is 2-add to tree

Step 3:

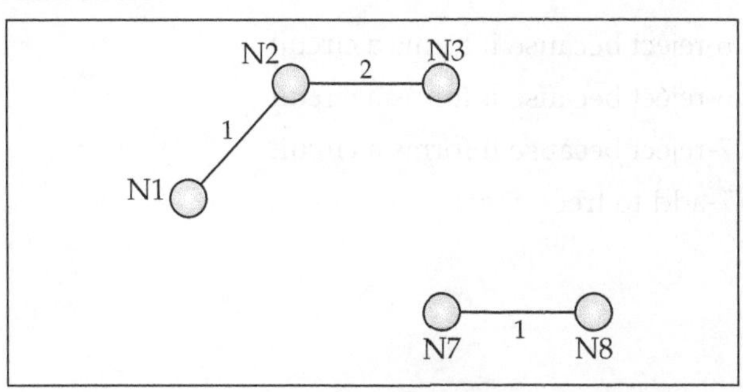

N_1 to N_6-cost is 3-add to tree

Step 4:

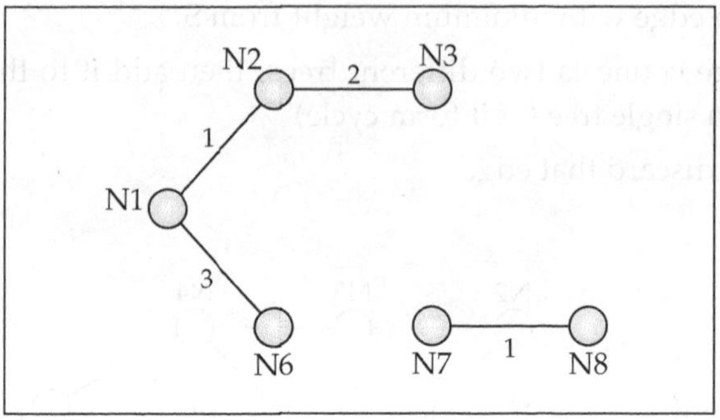

N_2 to N_6-cost is 4-reject because it forms a circuit

N_3 to N_4-cost is 4-add to tree

Step 5:

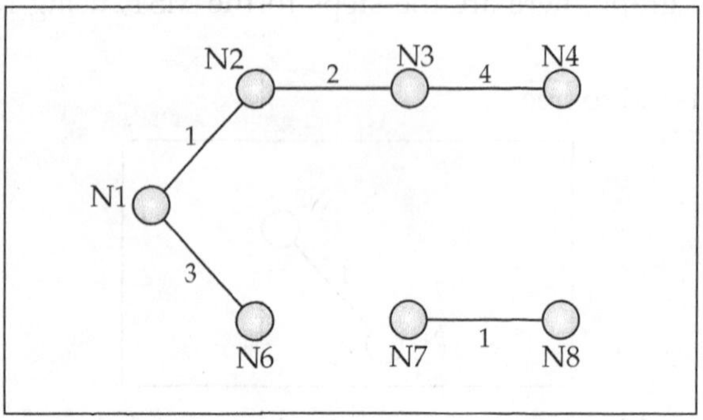

N_2 to N_7-cost is 5-add to tree

Step 6:

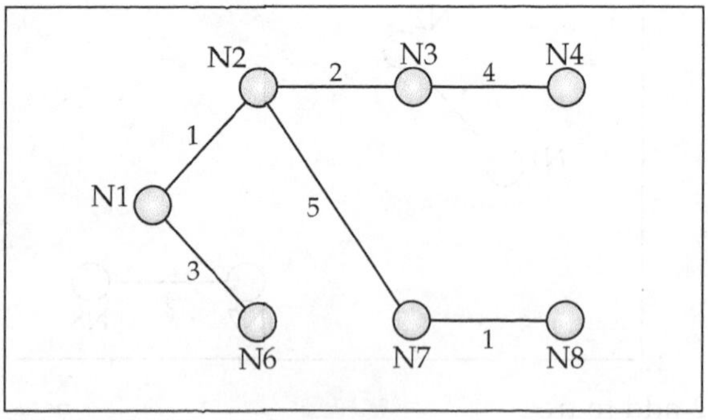

N_3 to N_7-cost is 6-reject because it forms a circuit

N_4 to N_8-cost is 6-reject because it forms a circuit

N_4 to N_7-cost is 7-reject because it forms a circuit

N_4 to N_5-cost is 7-add to tree

Step 7:

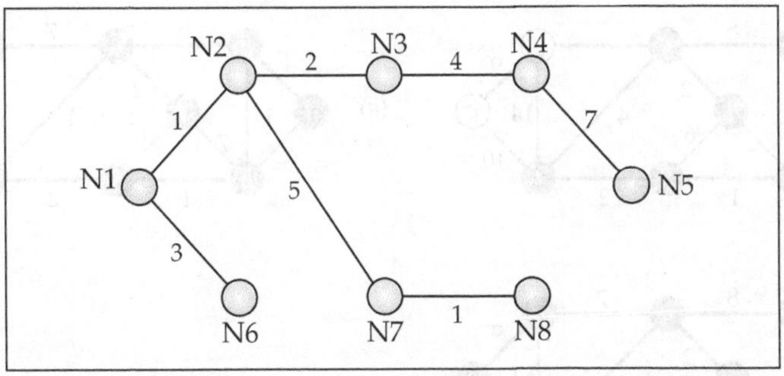

We stop here, because $n-1$ edges have been added. We are left with the minimum spanning tree, with a total weight of 23.

2. Prim's Algorithm: One of the classic algorithms for this problem is that found by Robert C. Prim. It's a **greedy** style algorithm and it's guaranteed to produce a correct result.

In the following discussion, let the distance from each node not in the tree to the tree be the edge of minimal weight between that node and some node in the tree. If there is no such edge, assume the distance is infinity (this shouldn't happen).

The algorithm (greedily) builds the minimal spanning tree by iteratively adding nodes into a working tree:

- Start with a tree which contains only one node.
- Identify a node (outside the tree) which is closest to the tree and add the minimum weight edge from that node to some node in the tree and incorporate the additional node as a part of the tree.
- If there are less than $n-1$ edges in the tree, go to 2.

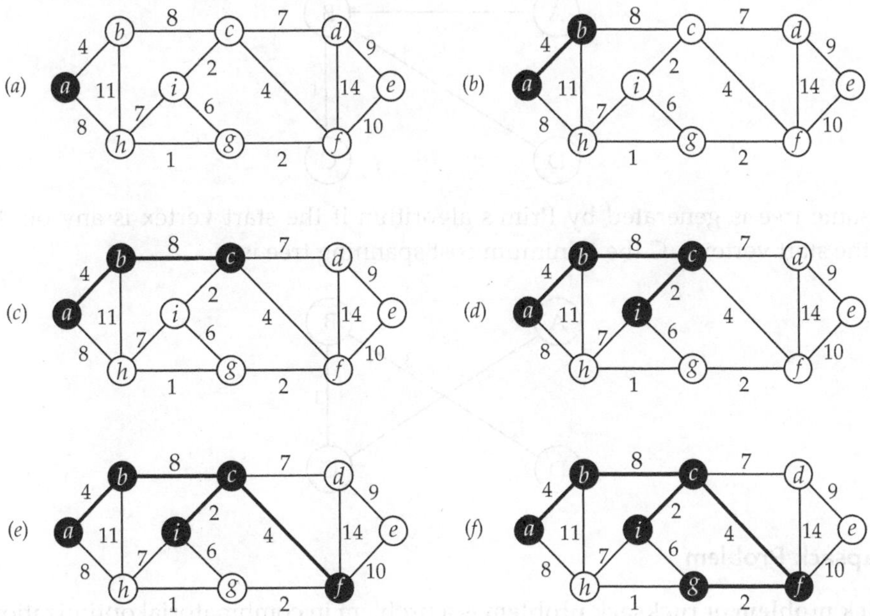

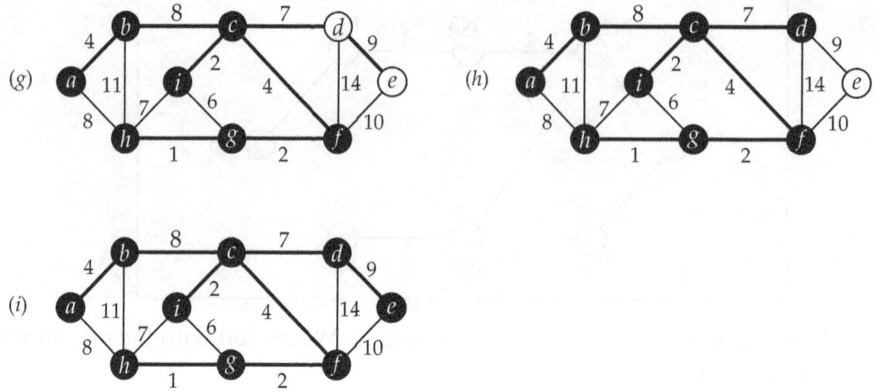

Note: It is not necessary that Prim's and Kruskal's algorithm generate the same minimum-cost spanning tree. For example, for the graph:

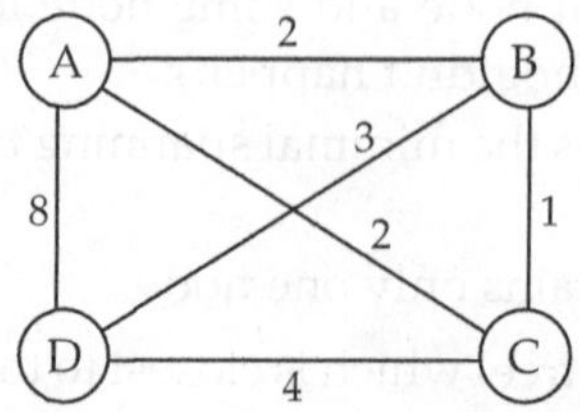

Kruskal's algorithm (that imposes an ordering on edges with equal weights) results in the following minimum cost spanning tree:

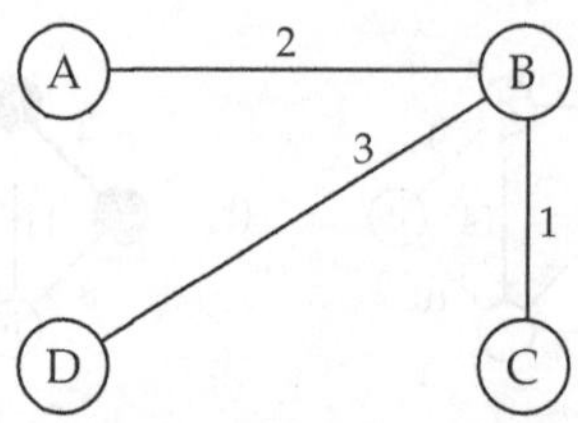

The same tree is generated by Prim's algorithm if the start vertex is any of: A, B, or D; however if the start vertex is C the minimum cost spanning tree is:

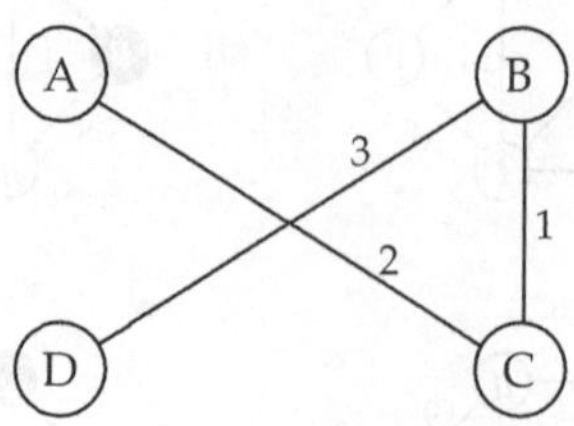

5.2.4 Knapsack Problem

The **knapsack problem** or **rucksack problem** is a problem in combinatorial optimization: Given a set of items, each with a weight and a value, determine the number of each item to include in a collection so that the total weight is less than a given limit and the total value is as large as possible. It derives its name from the problem faced by someone who is constrained by a fixed-size knapsack and must fill it with the most useful items.The problem often arises in resource allocation with financial constraints. With the help of greedy method we will solve **Fractional knapsack Problem** as following:

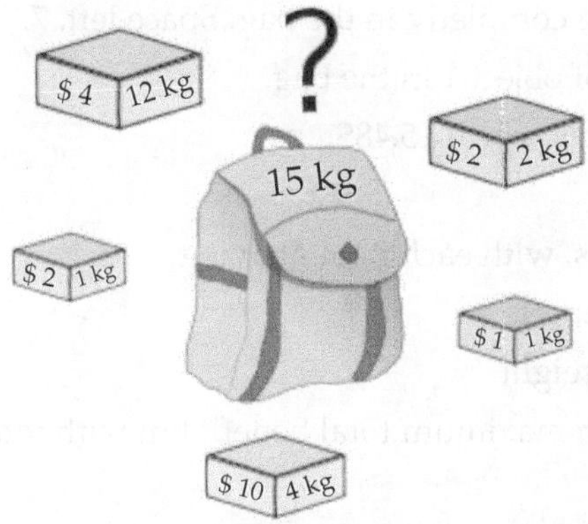

Fig. 5.2. Knapsack with Different Weights

The Problem: The Fractional Knapsack Problem usually say that: Thief has just broken into the Fort Knox! He sees himself in a room with n piles of gold dust. Because the each pile has a different purity, each pile also has a different value ($v[i]$) and a different weight ($c[i]$). Ted has a knapsack that can only hold W kilograms. Given n, v, c and W, calculate which piles Ted should completely put into his knapsack and which he should put only a fraction of.

So, for this input:

$$n = 5$$
$$c = \{12, 1, 2, 1, 4\}$$
$$v = \{4, 2, 2, 1, 10\}$$
$$W = 15$$

Ted should take piles 2, 3, 4 and 5 completely and about 58% of pile 1for maximum profit.

You're usually dealling with a knapsack problem when you're give the cost and the benefits of certain objects and asked to obtain the maximum benefit so that the sum of the costs is smaller than a given value. You've got the **fractional** knapsack problem when you can take fractions (as opposed to all or nothing) of the objects.

The Algorithm: This is a standard greedy algorithm. In fact, it's one of the classic examples. The idea is to calculate for each object the ratio of *value/cost*, and sort them according to this ratio. Then you take the objects with the highest ratios and add them until you can't add the next object as whole. Finally add as much as you can of the next object.

So, for our example:

$$v = \{4, 2, 2, 1, 10\}$$
$$c = \{12, 1, 2, 1, 4\}$$
$$r = \{1/3, 2, 1, 1, 5/2\}$$

From this it's obvious that you should add the objects: 5, 2, 3, 4 and then as much as possible of 1. The output of my programme is this:

Added object 5 (10$, 4Kg) completly in the bag. Space left: 11.

Added object 2 (2$, 1Kg) completly in the bag. Space left: 10.

Added object 3 (2$, 2Kg) completly in the bag. Space left: 8.

Added object 4 (1$, 1Kg) completly in the bag. Space left: 7.

Added 58% (4$, 12Kg) of object 1 in the bag.

Filled the bag with objects worth 15.48$.

Example:

Given: A set S of n items, with each item i having

– *bi-a* positive benefit

– *wi-a* positive weight

Goal: Choose items with maximum total benefit but with total weight at most W.

Item:

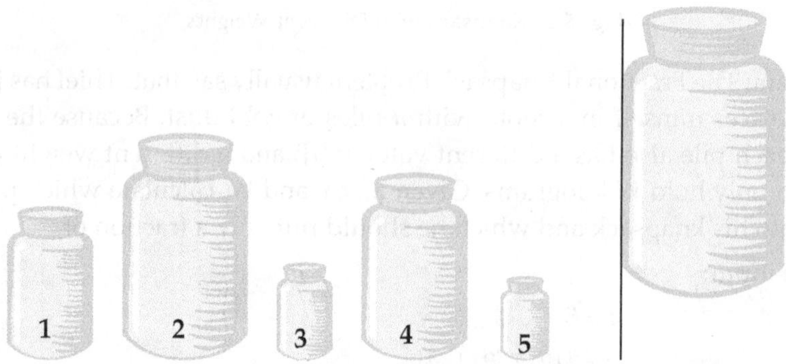

	1	2	3	4	5	
Weight	4ml	8ml	2ml	6ml	1ml	10ml
Profit:	12	32	40	30	50	
Value/ml	3	4	20	5	50	

Solution: 1ml of 5

2ml of 3

6ml of 4

1ml of 2

Algorithm for knapsack problem:

- Greedy choice: Keep taking item with highest **value** (benefit to weight ratio)

– Since

$$\sum_{i \in S} b_i(x_i/w_i) = \sum_{i \in S} b_i(x_i/w_i)x_i$$

Algorithm ***fractionalKnapsack*** **(S, W)**

Input: set S of items w/ benefit ***bi*** **and weight** ***wi*; max. weight W**

Output: amount ***xi*** **of each item** ***i*** **to maximize benefit w/ weight at most W**

```
for each item i in S
    xi ← 0
    vi ← bi/wi          {value}
w ← 0                   {total weight}
while w < W
    remove item i with highest vi
    xi ← min{wi , W-w}
    w ← w + min{wi , W-w}
```

5.2.5 Single Source Shortest Path

In this section, we consider the **single-source shortest path** problem: Single source shortest path problem is to find shortest path from a specific source vertex to every other vertex in weighted, directed graph. Given an edge-weighted graph G(V, E) and a vertex V0 in V, find the shortest weighted path from V0 to every other vertex in V. Why do we find the shortest path to every other vertex if we are interested only in the shortest path from, only source to destination? It turns out that in order to find the shortest path from source to destination it is necessary to find the shortest path from source to every other vertex in G! Clearly, when we search for the shortest path, we must consider all the vertices in V. If a vertex is ignored, say V*i*. then we will not consider any of the paths from source to destination that pass through V*i*. But if we fail to consider all the paths from source to destination, we cannot be assured of finding the shortest one.

Example:

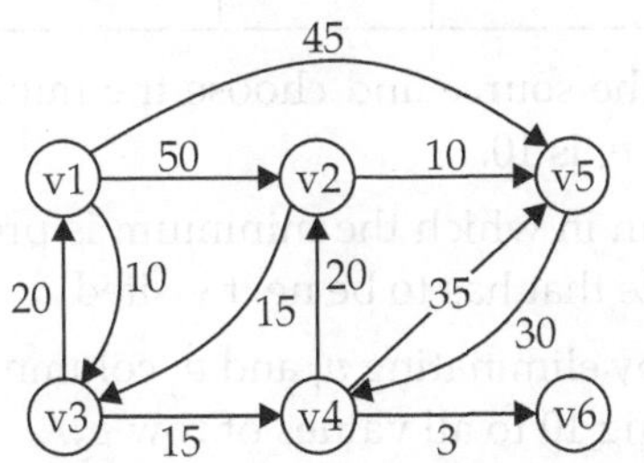

Consider the digraph in figure. Let the numbers on the edges be the costs of traveling along that route. If a person is interested travel from $v1$ to $v2$, then he encounters many paths. Some of them are:

1. $v1 -> v2$ = 50 units
2. $v1 -> v3 -> v4 -> v2$ = 10 + 15 + 20 = 45 units
3. $v1 -> v5 -> v4 -> v2$ = 45 + 30 + 20 = 95 units
4. $v1 -> v3 -> v4 -> v5 -> v4 -> v2$ = 10 +15 + 35 + 30 + 20 =110 units

The cheapest path among these is the path along *v*1à *v*3à *v*4à *v*2. The cost of the path is 10 + 15 + 20 = 45 units. Even though there are three edges on this path, it is cheaper than traveling along the path connecting *v*1 and *v*2 directly *i.e.,* the path *v*1à *v*2 that costs 50 units. One can also notice that, it is not possible to travel to *v*6 from any other node.

To formulate a greedy based algorithm to generate the cheapest paths, we must conceive a multistage solution to the problem and also of an optimization measure. One possibility is to build the shortest paths one by one. As an optimization measure we can use the sum of the lengths of all paths so far generated. For this measure to be minimized, each individual path must be of minimum length. If we have already constructed *i* shortest paths, then using this optimization measure, the next path to be constructed should be the next shortest minimum length path. The greedy way to generate these paths in non-decreasing order of path length. First, a shortest path to the nearest vertex is generated. Then a shortest path to the second nearest vertex is generated, and so on. A much simpler method would be to solve it using matrix representation. The steps that should be followed is as follows,

Step 1: find the adjacency matrix for the given graph. The adjacency matrix for above graph is given below

	V1	V2	V3	V4	V5	V6
V1	-	50	10	∞	45	∞
V2	∞	-	15	∞	10	∞
V3	20	∞	-	15	∞	∞
V4	∞	20	∞	-	35	∞
V5	∞	∞	∞	30	-	∞
V6	∞	∞	∞	3	∞	-

Step 2: consider v_1 to be the source and choose the minimum entry in the row v_1. In the above table the minimum in row v_1 is 10.

Step 3: find out the column in which the minimum is present, for the above example it is column *v*3. Hence, this is the node that has to be next visited.

Step 4: compute a matrix by eliminating v_1 and v_3 columns. Initially retain only row v_1. The second row is computed by adding 10 to all values of row v_3.

The resulting matrix is

	V2	V4	V5	V6
V1 ->Vw	50	∞	45	∞
V1 – >V3 – >Vw	∞ + 10	15 + 10	∞ + 10	∞ + 10
Minimum	50	25	45	∞

Step 5: find the minimum in each column. Now select the minimum from the resulting row. In the above example the minimum is 25. Repeat step 3 followed by step 4 till all vertices are covered or single column is left.

The solution for the above graph can be continued as follows

	V2	V5	V6
V1 – > Vw	50	45	∞
V1 – > V3 – >V4 – >Vw	25 + 20	25 + 35	25 + ∞
Minimum	45	45	∞

	V5	V6
V1 – > Vw	45	∞
V1– > V3 – > V4 – >V2 – >Vw	45 + 10	45 + ∞
Minimum	45	∞

	V6
V1 – > Vw	∞
V1 – >V3 – >V4 – >V2 – >V5 – >Vw	45 + ∞
Minimum	∞

Finally the cheapest path from *v*1 to all other vertices is given by

V1 – >V3 – > V4 – > V2 – > V5.

5.3 BRANCH AND BOUND

Branch and Bound is a technique to compute an optimal solution according to an arbitrary cost function and show how it is available in any problem. In other word we can say it is an organized and highly structured search of all possible solutions to a problem. It is mainly used for combinatorial and discrete global optimizations of problems. This technique is mainly used when we have very large problem space and all other algorithms fails. This technique is based on the enmasse elimination of the candidates. Basically Branch and Bound technique reduces whole number of possible candidates that are not just satisfactory and thus, won't contribute to optimal solution.

In Branch and Bound technique we insert some factors which convert complex BFS into simple search pattern. Instead of searching throughout the entire decision/search tree structure, it insert some sort of criteria, according to which the complexity of the BFS can be reduced. We can do this by adding "costs."

We can move through this tree based on the costs; a node is a more possible candidate toward the solution if its cost is less than other nodes. What we did is add an essence of depth-search to the breadth-first meaning; there is going to be a priority queue, according to which we are running the breath-first search. The traditional BFS runs from left to right, but now we'll have the priority queue instead.

The beauty of this approach is that we haven't lost the not-so-possible candidates. You see, they are stored somewhere on the end of the priority queue, so this algorithm doesn't neglect the rest of the possible options. Summing these up, this is in fact a typical Branch and Bound algorithm technique.

B and B is composed of two main actions, but there's an additional step. The first step is, as its name suggests, the ***branching***. This is where we define the tree structure from the set of candidates in a recursive manner. The second action is called ***bounding*** since this procedure calculates the upper and lower bounds of each node from the tree.

Furthermore, there's the additional ***pruning*** step that we can add. In a nutshell, it means that if the lower bound for some node of the tree is greater than the upper bound of some other node of the tree, then the first node of the tree can be "discarded" (remember, it does not mean eliminate) from the search. A variable always holds the value of the global minimum upper bound.

Terminology

Definition 1: ***Live node*** is a node that has been generated but whose children have not yet been generated.

Definition 2: ***E-node*** is a live node whose children are currently being explored. In other words, an E-node is a node currently being expanded.

Definition 3: ***Dead node*** is a generated node that is not to be expanded or explored any further. All children of a dead node have already been expanded.

Definition 4: ***Branch-and-bound*** refers to all state space search methods in which all children of an E-node are generated before any other live node can become the E-node.

- Both BFS and DFS generalize to branch-and-bound strategies
  - BFS is an FIFO search in terms of live nodes, where we put list of live nodes in queue.
  - DFS is an LIFO search in terms of live nodes, where we put list of live nodes in stack.

Just like backtracking, we will use bounding functions to avoid generating sub-trees that do not contain an answer node

Example: 4-queens

- **FIFO branch-and-bound algorithm**
  - Initially, there is only one live node; no queen has been placed on the chessboard.
  - The only live node becomes E-node.
  - Expand and generate all its children; children being a queen in column 1, 2, 3, and 4 of row 1 (only live nodes left).
  - Next E-node is the node with queen in row 1 and column 1

— Expand this node, and add the possible nodes to the queue of live nodes

— Bound the nodes that become dead nodes

- **Least Cost (LC) search**

Selection rule does not give preference to nodes that will lead to answer quickly but just queues those behind the current live nodes. In 4-queen problem, if three queens have been placed on the board, it is obvious that the answer may be reached in one more move. The rigid selection rule requires that other live nodes be expanded and then, the current node be tested.

- Rank the live nodes by using a heuristic $\hat{c}(\cdot)$
- The next E-node is selected on the basis of this ranking function
- Heuristic is based on the expected additional computational effort (cost) to reach a solution from the current live node
- For any node x, the cost could be given by:

1. Number of nodes in sub-tree x that need to be generated before an answer can be reached, Search will always generate the minimum number of nodes.
2. Number of levels to the nearest answer node in the subtree x (root) for 4-queen problem is 4.

5.4 KNAPSACK PROBLEM USING BRANCH AND BOUND

The Knapsack problem is a combinatorial optimization problem. You are given a set of items, each with its own cost and value, and you are to determine the number of each item that you should pack into the knapsack so that the total cost doesn't exceed the given limitation, but the total value is as high as possible. As you can see, this is a maximization problem; it is part of combinatory and applied mathematics.

The value is the weight of the items, and their cost represents how much the item is worth. The knapsack can hold a specified amount of weight, and this limitation cannot be exceeded. In short, you want to maximize the storage capability of the knapsack by packing the most valuable items in it. Sometimes this problem is told in the form of a robbery. Obviously, the thief wants the best bang for his buck (his effort).

Let's say the weight of the items are $W_1, W_2, \ldots W_k, \ldots W_n$ and their cost is $C_1, C_2, \ldots C_k, \ldots C_n$, respectively; the capacity of the knapsack is specified as K. Now we have the following mathematical formula to calculate the upper bound [UB]. Check it out!

$$\text{UB} = current - value + \sum_{j=i+1}^{k-1} cj + (K - total - sum) \times \frac{c_k}{w_k}$$

Right after this point we can already present the pseudo-code of the algorithm.

Procedure knapsack:

```
Initialize root;
        PQ <- root;
```

```
        max_cost := root.cost;
        while PQ not equal do
        current <- PQ;
        if (current.bound > max_cost) then
           create left_child := next item;
              if (left_child.cost > max_cost)
                 max_cost := left_child.cost;
                 update best_solution;
              end if;
           if (left_child.bound > max_cost)
           PQ <- left_child;
        end if;
        create right_child; // it skips packing the next item
        if (right_child.bound > max_cost)
        PQ <- right_child;
        end if;
   end if;
   end while;
   return best_solution and its cost;
   end procedure;
```

Consider of size **K** and we want to select from a set of *n* objects , where the ith object has size s_i and value v_i, a subset of these objects to maximize the value contained in the knapsack with the contents of the knapsack less than or equal to K.

Suppose that K = 16 and n = 4, and we have the following set of objects ordered by their value density.

i	v_i	s_i	v_i/s_i
1	$45	3	$15
2	$30	5	$ 6
3	$45	9	$ 5
4	$10	5	$ 2

We will construct the state space where each node contains the total current value in the knapsack, the total current size of the contents of the knapsack, and maximum potential value that the knapsack can hold. In the algorithm, we will also keep a record of the maximum value of any node (partially or completely filled knapsack) found so far. When we perform the depth-first traversal of the state-space tree, a node is "promising" if its maximum potential value is greater than this current best value.

We begin the state space tree with the root consisting of the empty knapsack. The current weight and value are obviously 0. To find the maximum potential value we treat the problem as if it were the fractional knapsack problem and we were using the greedy algorithmic solution to that problem. We have shown that the greedy approach to the fractional knapsack problem yields an optimal solution. We place each of the remaining objects, in turn, into the knapsack until the next selected object is too big to fit into the knapsack. We then use the fractional amount of that object that could be placed in the knapsack to determine the maximum potential value.

totalSize = current Size + size of remaining objects that can be fully placed

bound (maximum potential value) = current Value + value of remaining objects fully placed + (K - total Size) * (value density of item that is partially placed)

In general, for a node at level *i* in the state space tree (the first *i* items have been considered for selection) and for the kth object as the one that will not completely fit into the remaining space in the knapsack, these formulae can be written:

$$\text{Total Size} = \text{currentSize} + \sum_{j=i+1}^{k+1} sj$$

$$\text{Bound} = \text{current Value} + \sum_{j=i+1}^{k+1} vj + (\text{K} - \text{totalSize}) * (v_k/s_k)$$

For the root node, current Size = 0, current Value = 0

total Size = $0 + s_1 + s_2 = 0 + 3 + 5 = 8$

bound = $0 + v_1 + v_2 + (\text{K} - \text{total Size}) * (v_3/s_3) = 0 + \$45 + \$30 + (16 - 8) * (\$5)$
$= \$75 + \$40 = \$115$

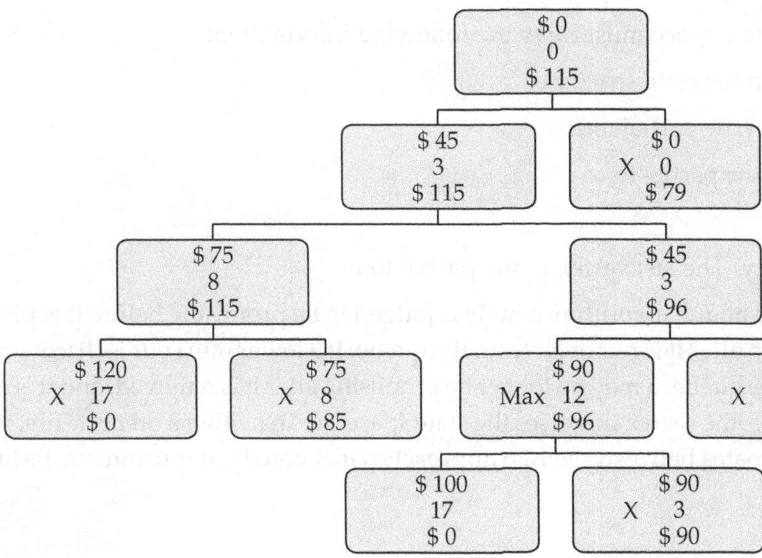

The computation of the bound and the selection criteria for promising nodes is the same as before. We must replace the depth-first traversal of the state space tree with a breadth first traversal. In the depth-first traversal the auxiliary data structure used to store Nodes was (implicitly) the stack. In breath-first traversal, the auxiliary data structure is explicitly the queue. For example, problem this algorithm traverses the following state space:

5.5 TRAVELING SALESPERSON PROBLEM

Instead of using a Queue to perform a breadth-first traversal of the state space, we will use a Priority-Queue and perform a "best-first" traversal. For the TSP we first compute the minimum possible tour by finding the minimum edge exiting each vertex. The sum of these edges may not (most likely don't) form a possible tour, but since every vertex must be visited once and only once, every vertex must be exited once. Therefore, no tour can be shorter than the sum of these minimum edges.

At each subsequent node, the lower bound for a "tour in progress" is the length of the tour to that point plus the sum of the minimum edge exiting the end vertex of the partial tour and each of the minimum edges leaving all of the remaining unvisited vertices. If this bound is less than the current minimum tour, the node is "promising" and the node is added to the queue. Initially the minTour is set to infinity. When a node whose path includes all of the vertices except one is reviewed there is only one possible way for the tour to complete. The remaining vertex and the first are added to the path and the length of the tour is the current length plus the length of the edge to the remaining vertex and the length of the edge from there back to the starting vertex. If this tour length is better than the current minimum, it becomes the minimum tour length. Once a first complete tour is discovered, nodes whose bound are greater than or equal to this minTour are deemed "non-promising" and are pruned.

The nodes in state space must carry the following information:

- Their level in the state space tree
- The length of the partial tour
- The path of the partial tour
- The bound
- (for efficiency) The last vertex in the partial tour

In a branch and bound algorithm, a node is judged to be promising before it is placed in the queue and tested again after it is removed from the queue. If a lower minTour is discovered during the time a node is in the queue, it may no longer be promising after it is removed, and it is discarded. Using a Priority Queue, the search traverses the state space tree in neither a breadth-first nor depth-first fashion, but alternates between the two approaches in a greedy, opportunistic fashion.

Example:

Let G be a fully connected directed graph containing five vertices that is represented by the following adjacency list:

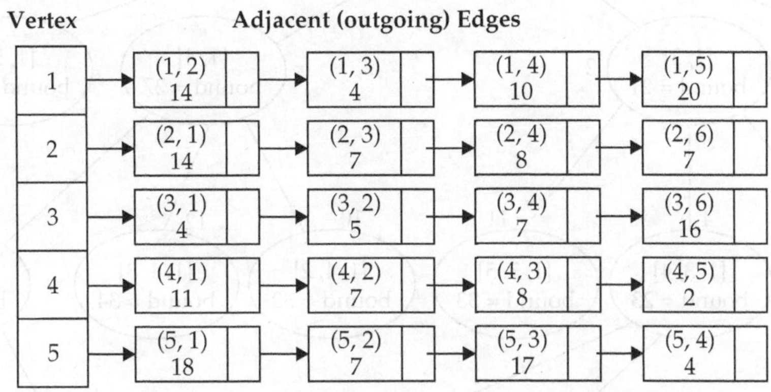

We assume in the implementation of this algorithm that vertices are labeled by an integer number and edges contain the source and sink vertices and a cost or length label. The tour will start at vertex 1, and the initial bound for the minimum tour is the sum of the minimum outgoing edges from each vertex.

Vertex 1 min (14, 4, 10, 20) = 4

Vertex 2 min (14, 7, 8, 7) = 7

Vertex 3 min (4, 5, 7, 16) = 4

Vertex 4 min (11, 7, 9, 2) = 2

Vertex 5 min (18, 7, 17, 4) = 4

Bound = 21

Since the bound for this node (21) is less than the initial minTour (∞), nodes for all of the adjacent vertices are added to the state space tree at level 1. The bound for the node for the partial tour from 1 to 2 is determined to be:

bound = length from 1 to 2 + sum of min outgoing edges for vertices 2 to 5
= 14 + (7 + 4 + 2 + 4) = 31

After each new node is added to the Priority-Queue, the node with the best bound is removed and similarly processed. The algorithm terminates when the queue is empty.

Note that the node for the state with a partial tour from [1, 2] is the second node placed in the priority queue, but the 8th node to be removed. By the time it is removed and examined, a tour of length 30 (which turns out to be the optimal tour) has already been discovered, and, since its bound exceeds this length, it is discarded without having to check any of the possible tours that extend it.

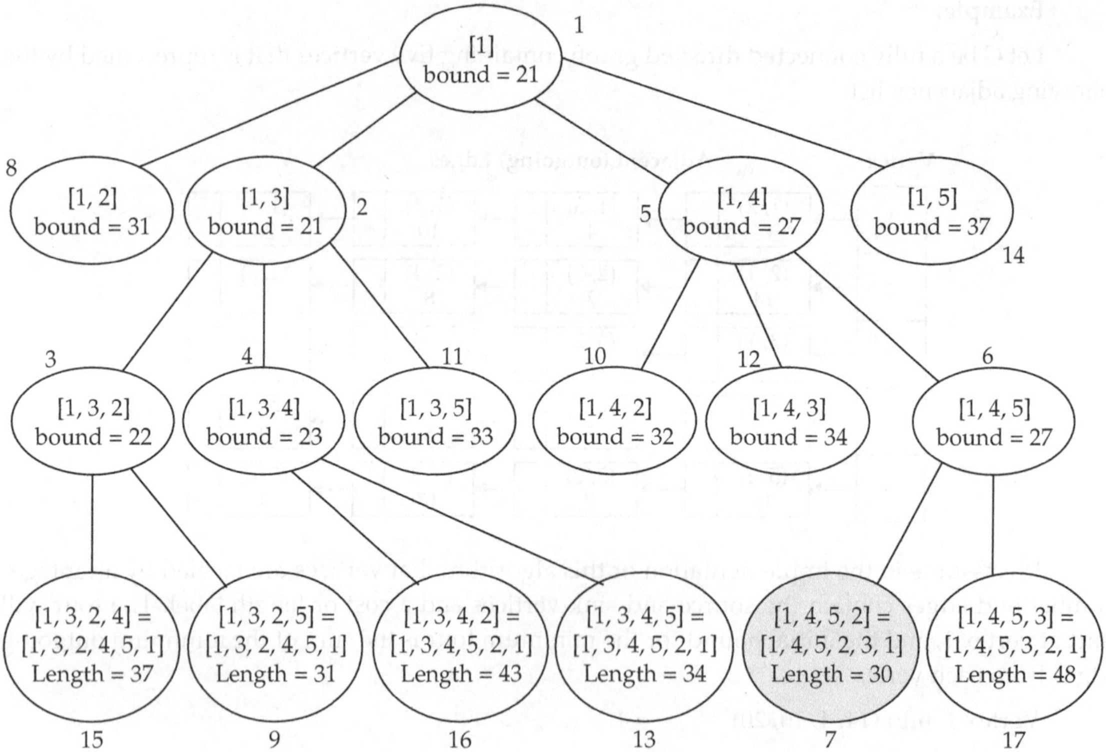

SUMMARY

Greedy algorithms **do not always** yield a genuinely optimal solution. In such cases the greedy method is frequently the basis of a *heuristic approach*. ·Even for problems which can be solved exactly by a greedy algorithm, establishing the **correctness** of the method may be a non-trivial process. Branch and Bound is a general search method. Suppose we wish to minimize a function $f(x)$, where x is restricted to some feasible region (defined, *e.g.*, by explicit mathematical constraints). To apply branch and bound, one must have a means of computing a lower bound on an instance of the optimization problem and a means of dividing the feasible region of a problem to create smaller sub-problems. There must also be a way to compute an upper bound (feasible solution) for at least some instances; for practical purposes, it should be possible to compute upper bounds for some set of nontrivial feasible regions.

EXERCISE

1. What is Greedy method?
2. Define Prim's algorithm.
3. Define Kruskal's algorithm.
4. Define Dijikstra's shortest path algorithm.
5. What are the applications of spanning trees?
6. Define Branch and Bound method.

7. Define Knapsack's problem.
8. Define Travelling salesman problem.
9. What are the applications of branch and bound?
10. Solve the 0/1 knapsack problem $n = 3$, $(w_1, w_2, w_3) = (2, 3, 3)$, $(p_1, p_2, p_3) = (1, 2, 4)$ and $m = 6$ find optimal solution.
11. Consider the knapsack instance $n = 3$, $(w_1, w_2, w_3) = (2, 3, 4)$ and $(p_1, p_2, p_3) = (1, 2, 5)$, $m = 5$. find the optimal solution.
12. Solve the 4 queens problem using branch and bound.
13. Solve the instance of the knapsack problem below. Capacity W= 5

Item	*Weight*	*Value*
1	2	\$12
2	1	\$10
3	3	\$20
4	2	\$15

14. Solve the TSP problem having the following cost matrix using branch and bound techniques.

	A	B	C	D
A	[x	5	2	3]
B	[4	x	2	3]
C	[4	2	x	3]
D	[7	6	8	x]

15. Solve the following Activity scheduling problem?

(i)

Task	A	B	C	D	E	F	G	H	I	J
Start Time	1	2	3	4	5	6	7	8	9	10
End Time	5	3	4	6	7	8	11	10	12	13

(ii)

Task	A	B	C	D	E	F	G	H	I	J
Start Time	1	2	3	4	7	8	9	9	11	12
End Time	3	5	4	7	10	9	11	13	12	14

Chapter 6 DYNAMIC PROGRAMMING

6.1 INTRODUCTION

Dynamic programming is a stage-wise search method suitable for optimization problems whose solutions may be viewed as the result of a sequence of decisions. The most attractive property of this strategy is that during the search for a solution it avoids full enumeration by pruning early partial decision solutions that cannot possibly lead to optimal solution. In many practical situations, this strategy hits the optimal solution in a polynomial number of decision steps. However, in the worst case, such a strategy may end up performing full enumeration. Dynamic programming takes advantage of the duplication and arranges to solve each sub-problem only once, saving the solution (in table or something) for later use. The underlying idea of dynamic programming is: avoid calculating the same stuff twice, usually by keeping a table of known results of sub-problems. Unlike divide-and-conquer, which solve the sub-problems top-down, a dynamic programming is a bottom-up technique.

Bottom-up means

(*i*) Start with the smallest sub-problems.

(*ii*) Combining theirs solutions obtain the solutions to sub-problems of increasing size.

(*iii*) Until arrive at the solution of the original problem.

6.2 CHARACTERISTICS OF DYNAMIC PROGRAMMING

There are a number of characteristics that are common to these two problems and to all dynamic programming problems. These are:

1. The problem can be divided into *stages* with a *decision* required at each stage. In the capital budgeting problem the stages were the allocations to a single plant. The decision was how much to spend. In the shortest path problem, they were defined by the structure of the graph. The decision was to go next.
2. Each stage has a number of *states* associated with it. The states for the capital budgeting problem corresponded to the amount spent at that point in time. The states for the shortest path problem were the node reached.

3. The decision at one stage transforms one state into a state in the next stage. The decision of how much to spend gave a total amount spent for the next stage. The decision of where to go next defined where you arrived in the next stage.
4. Given the current state, the optimal decision for each of the remaining states does not depend on the previous states or decisions. In the budgeting problem, it is not necessary to know how the money was spent in previous stages, only how much was spent. In the path problem, it was not necessary to know how you got to a node, only that you did.
5. There exists a recursive relationship that identifies the optimal decision for stage j, given that stage $j + 1$ has already been solved.
6. The final stage must be solvable by itself.

The last two properties are tied up in the recursive relationships given above. The big skill in dynamic programming, and the art involved, is to take a problem and determine stages and states so that all of the above hold. If you can, then the recursive relationship makes finding the values relatively easy.

6.3 DIVIDE AND CONQUER V/S DYNAMIC PROGRAMMING

In divide and conquer methodology sub-problems are independent. In this case, we solve sub-problems independently and recursively so some sub-problems solved repeatedly while in dynamic programming sub-problems are dependent. Every sub-problem solved at once and solution of that sub-problem stored in table to solve higher level sub-problems.

6.4 THE PRINCIPLE OF OPTIMALITY

The dynamic programming relies on a principle of optimality. This principle states that in an optimal sequence of decisions or choices, each subsequence must also be optimal. For example, in matrix chain multiplication problem, not only the value we are interested in is optimal but all the other entries in the table are also representing optimal.

The principle can be related as follows: the optimal solution to a problem is a combination of optimal solutions to some of its sub-problems.

The difficulty in turning the principle of optimally into an algorithm is that it is not usually obvious which sub-problems are relevant to the problem under consideration.

6.5 MATRIX CHAIN MULTIPLICATION

The *Chain Matrix Multiplication Problem* is stated as follows: "Given a sequence A_1, A_2 . . . An and dimensions p_0, p_1 . . . pn where Ai is of dimension $pi - 1 \times pi$, determine the order of multiplication that minimizes the number of operations ".

If there are n items, there are $n - 1$ ways in which outer most pair of parentheses can placed.

$(A_1)(A_2 A_3 A_4 \dots A_n)$

or $(A_1A_2)(A_3A_4 \dots A_n)$

or $(A_1A_2A_3)(A_4 \dots A_n)$

......

or $(A_1A_2A_3A_4 \dots A_n - 1)(A_n)$

Once we split just after the kth matrix, we create two sub-lists to be parenthesized, one with k and other with $n - k$ matrices. $(A_1A_2 \dots A_k)$ $(A_k + 1 \dots A_n)$.

Thus, order of matrix multiplication can change the number of multiplication many times. How many possible distributions of brackets are there to try out?

$$T(n) = \sum_{i=1}^{n-1} T(i)\,T(n-i)$$

The solution is a huge number (exponential in terms of metrices: $t(n) = \Omega(2^n)$; it is equal to the number of binary tree with n leaves which is easy to see that it is exponential. Thus, we cannot check them all. So what do we do? Eliminate repetitions in the calculation, and avoid calculations!!!! These different distributions of brackets significantly overlap!

We apply the technique to build the table of optimal distribution of brackets for all sequence A_i .... A_j, Such that in the mth row we have all optimal distribution of brackets for all sequences A_i .... A_j, for $j - i = m >= 2$. in order to find optimal distribution for sequence A_i ..... A_j of length $j - i = m + 1$ we consider all split $(A_1 \dots\dots A_k)(A_k + 1 \dots\dots A_j)$ for all $k, = i <= j$ and use the table for $k - i$ and $j - (k + 1)$ which have already been calculated.

Example:

Let A be an n by m matrix, let B be an m by p matrix, then C = AB is an n by p matrix. C = AB can be computed as $O(nmp)$ time, using traditional matrix multiplication. Suppose, we want to compute $A_1A_2A_3A_4$. Matrix multiplication is associative, so we can do the multiplication in several different orders.

- A_1 is 10 by 100 matrix
- A_2 is 100 by 5 matrix
- A_3 is 5 by 50 matrix
- $A_1A_2A_3A_4$ is 10 by 50 matrix.

If we calculate $M = (M_1M_2)M_3$, then the number of scalar multiplications is:

	$10 * 100 * 5$ to multiply $K = M_1M_2$.	Dimension of K is 10×5.
+	$10 * 5 * 50$ to multiply $M = KM_3$.	Dimension of M is 10×50.

Total: 7,500 scalar multiplications.

If we calculate $M = M_1(M_2M_3)$ then the number of scalar multiplications is:

	$100 * 5 * 50$ to multiply $L = M_2M_3$.	Dimension of L is 100×50.
+	$10 * 100 * 50$ to multiply $M = M_1L$.	Dimension of M is 10×50.

Total: 75,000 scalar multiplications.

Therefore, the **problem** boils down to: given a product chain of N matrices, fully parenthesize the chain in order to minimize the number of scalar multiplications.

A solution: brute force method using dynamic programming, *i.e.*, write and implement a dynamic programming formula to solve the problem.

A dynamic programming formula is always recursive. It can be implemented as:

1. Plain recursive code (top down)
2. Memorized code (*i.e.*, recursive code with storage, top down)
3. Iterative code (bottom up)

***m* [*i,j*]** is the number of scalar multiplications needed to multiply matrices $M_i M_{i+1} M_{i+2} \cdots M_j$. Each matrix M_k has dimension $p_{k-1} \times p_k$. Dimensions of all matrices are stored in array $P = < p_0\ p_1 \ldots p_N >$. $i = 1, \ldots n, j = 1, \ldots n.$

$$m\ [i, j] = \begin{cases} 0 & if\ i = j \\ \min\ (m[i, k] + m[k+1, j] + p_{i+1} * p_k * p_j) & if\ i < j \\ \text{for all } k\ i \le k < j & \end{cases}$$

Algorithm Matrix Chain Multiplication.

```
MATRIX-CHAIN-ORDER(P)
{
        n=length(P)-1
        //length[P]=N+1
        for i=1to n do
              m[i,i]=0
        for L=2 to n do
              for i=1 to n - L + 1 do
                    j=i+L-1
                    m[i,j]=∞
                    for k=I to j - 1 do
                          q=m[i,k]+m[k+1,j]+p_{i-1} p_k p_j
                          if q < m[i,j] then
                          m[i,j]=q
                          s[i,j]=k
                    end if
                end for
            end for
          end for
     return m and s
 }
```

Order of filling m matrix for $n = 4$ (*i.e.*, m_{11} is filled first, then m_{22}, then m_{33}, then m_{44}, then m_{12}, etc.)

Solved Example:

Given six metrics A_1 (30 × 35) A_2 (35 × 15) A_3 (15 × 5) A_4 (5 × 10) A_5 (10 × 20) A_6 (20 × 25)

According to Algorithm we know $P_0 = 30$, $P_1 = 35$, $P_2 = 15$, $P_3 = 5$, $P_4 = 10$, $P_5 = 20$, $P_6 = 25$

When N = 6

For $i = 1$ to 6

$m[1, 1] = 0$

for $t = 2$ to 6

for $i = 1$ to 5

$j = 2$

$m[1, 2] = \infty$

for $k = 1$ to 1

do $q = m[1, 1] + m[2, 2] + p_0 p_1 p_2 (30 * 35 * 15)$

$q = 15750$

$m[1, 2] = 15750$

$s[1, 2] = 1$

$m[2, 2] = 0$

⟶ Now $t = 2, j = 3, i = 2$

$m[2,3] = \infty$

$k = 2$ to 2

$q = m[2, 2] + m[3, 3] + p_1 p_2 p_3 (35 * 15 * 5)$

$q = 2625$

$m[2, 3] = 2625$

$m[2, 3] = 2$

⟶ Now $t = 2, i = 3, j = 4$

$m[3, 4] = \infty$

$k = 3$ to 3

$q = m[3, 3] + m[4, 4] + p_2 p_3 p_4 (15 * 5 * 10)$

$q = 750$

$m[3, 4] = 750$

$s[3, 4] = 3$

⟶ Now $t = 2, i = 4, j = 5$

$m[4, 5] = \infty$

$k = 4$ to 4

$Q = m[4, 4] + m[5, 5] + p_3 p_4 p_5 (5 * 10 * 20)$

Q = 1000

$m[4, 5] = 1000$

$s[4, 5] = 4$

⟶ Now $t = 2, \quad i = 5, \quad j = 6$

$m[5, 6] = \infty$

$k = 5$ to 5

$q = m[5, 5] + m[6, 6] + p_4 p_5 p_6$

$q = 5000$

$m[5, 6] = 5000$

$m\ [5, 6] = 5$

⟶ Now $t = 3, \quad i = 1, j = 3$

$m[1, 3] = \infty$

For $k = 1$ to 2

For $k = 1$

$q = m[1, 1] + m[2, 3] + p_0 p_1 p_3\ (30 * 35 * 5)$

$q = 2625 + 5250$

$q = 7875$

$q = m[1, 2] + m[3, 3] + p_0 p_1 p_3\ (30 * 15 * 5)$

$q = 15750 + 2250$

$q = 18000$

min(7875, 18000)

$m[1, 3] = 7875$

$s[1, 3] = 1$

⟶ Now $t = 3, \quad i = 2, \quad j = 4$

$m[2, 4] = \infty$

For $k = 2$ to 3

For $k = 2$

$q = m[2, 2] + m[3, 4] + p_1 p_2 p_4 (35 * 15 * 10)$

$q = 750 + 5250$

$q = 6000$

For $k = 3$

$q = m[2, 3] + m[4, 4] + p_1 p_3 p_4$

$q = 2625 + 1750$

$q = 4375$

min = (6000, 4375)

$m[2, 4] = 4375$

$S[2, 4] = 3$

By solving for all values we will get following data on the basis of calculation

15175	10500	5375	3500	5000	0
11875	7125	2500	1000	0	
9375	4375	750	0		
7875	2625	0			
15750	0				
0					

Principal Split points. k *i.e.*, A_i …….. $A_j = (A_i$ ….. $A_k)(A_k + 1$ ……… $A_j)$ is

3	3	3	5	5	0
3	3	3	4	0	
3	3	3	0		
1	2	0			
1	0				
0					

After all these calculations we found how to parenthesized matrix so it give optimum solution. For this purpose we will use following algorithm

```
Algorithm Optimum(s,i,j)
If i=j then
   Print Ai
Else Print "("
   Optimum(s,i,s[i,j])
   Optimum(s,s[i,j]+1,j)
   Print ")"
```

```
At our last pass i=1 and j=6
So Optimum(s,1,6)
```
Pass1-> `i≠j so`
```
Print "("
Optimum(s,1,3)
Optimum(s,4,6)
)
```
Pass2-> `i=1,j=3`

```
i≠j so print "("
  optimum(s,1,1)
  optimum(s,2,3)
  ")"
Pass3-> i=1,j=1
  Print A1
Pass 4-> i=2,j=3
  i≠j so print "("
  Optimum(s,2,2)
  Optimum(s.3,3)
  ")"
Pass5-> i=2,j=2
  Print A2
Pass6-> i=3,j=3
  Print A3
Pass7-> i=4,j=6
  i≠j so print "("
  optimum(s,4,5)
  optimum(s,6,6)
  ")"
Pass 8-> i=4,j=5
  i≠j so print "("
  optimum(s,4,4)
  optimum(s,5,5)
  ")"
Pass9-> i=4,j=4
  Print A4
Pass10-> i=5,j=5
  Print A5
Pass 11-> i=6,j=6
  Print A6
```

6.6 TRAVELING SALESMAN PROBLEM

The Traveling Salesman Problem (TSP) is a deceptively simple combinatorial problem. It can be stated very simply:

A salesman spends his time visiting n cities (or nodes) cyclically. In one tour he visits each city just once, and finishes up where he started. In what order should he visit them to minimize the distance traveled?

Many TSP's are *symmetric*—that is, for any two cities A and B, the distance from A to B is the same as that from B to A. In this case you will get exactly the same tour length if you reverse the order in which they are visited—so there is no need to distinguish between a tour and its reverse, and you can leave off the arrows on the tour diagram.

If there are only 2 cities then the problem is trivial, since only one tour is possible. For the symmetric case a 3 city TSP is also trivial. If all links are present then there are $(n - 1)!$ different tours for an n city asymmetric TSP. To see why this is so, pick any city as the first - then there are $n - 1$ choices for the second city visited, $n - 2$ choices for the third, and so on. For the symmetric case there are half as many distinct solutions—$(n - 1)!/2$ for an n city TSP. In either case the number of solutions becomes extremely large for large n, so that an exhaustive search is impracticable.

The general form of TSP problem was considered by mathematicians in the 1930's. During 1950's and 1960's it gained popularity in scientific circles. Researchers from RAND Corporation create a method to optimally solve TSP for 49 cities. In 1972, Karp proves that TSP is NP complete.

Application of TSP

- Transportation
  - — School Bus Routes
  - — Traveling Salesman
- Technology
  - — Microchip Manufacturing
  - — Network Engineering
- Biological
  - — Genome Sequencing

Solution to TSP

There are a few general methods for finding solutions for the TSP:

- Brute Force
- Dynamic Programming
- Approximation

Brute force: One way to solve this problem (and any other NP-complete problem) is to enumerate all possible routes, of which there are 10! (3,628,800) for 10 towns, and then choose the shortest. This is a ***brute force* algorithm**. It would only take a couple seconds on a typical PC to compute all the possible routes and distances for 10 towns. And you would only need to do it once. If we can compute a billion possible solution per second to solve the 30 stop than TSP will require more than 8×10^{15} years or 8 quadrillion years.

Example of TSP

In this example 5 different cities are given. Here matrix is representing different distance from one city to another. Solve it for minimum distance travel to salesman between these cities.

	1	2	3	4	5
1	—	5	9	8	7
2	8	—	10	6	14
3	12	9	—	14	11
4	13	4	6	—	3
5	4	7	13	9	—

- Find the Minimum distance in each row. $\Sigma r_i = 5 + 6 + 9 + 3 + 4 = 27$
- Subtract that minimum distance from each element of row.

	1	2	3	4	5
1	—	0	4	3	2
2	2	—	4	0	8
3	3	0	—	5	2
4	10	1	3	—	0
5	0	3	9	5	—

- Find the minimum of column. $\Sigma C_{j=}\ 0 + 0 + 3 + 0 + 0 = 3$
- Subtract that minimum distance from each element of column.

	1	2	3	4	5
1	—	0	1	3	2
2	2	—	1	0	8
3	3	0	—	5	2
4	10	1	0	—	0
5	0	3	6	5	—

- $B_{node} = \Sigma r_i + \Sigma C_j$

  $= 27 + 3$

  $= 30$

- Find the location of zero element in matrix.

  {(P, Q) } = {(1, 2) (2, 4) (3, 2) (4, 3) (4, 5) (5, 1)}

Now Compute $L(p, q) = Rp + Cq$ (Sum of minimum element of row and column)

(1, 2) = 1st row + 2nd column

$= 1 + 0$

$= 1$

(2, 4) = 2nd row + 4th column

$= 1 + 3$

$= 4$

(3, 2) = 3rd row + 2nd column

$= 2 + 0$

$= 2$

(4, 3) = 4th row + 3rd column
= 0 + 1
= 1
(4, 5) = 4th row + 5th column
= 0 + 2
= 2
(5,1) = 5th row + 1st column
= 3 + 2
= 5
= {1, 4, 2, 1, 2, 5}

The maximum of this L(*p*, *q*) is 5

- A barred node $\overline{(5, 1)}$ is to be created to be created to the left of Bnode. Hence the lower bound for this barred node is:

30 + 5 = 35 (Now delete row 5 and column 1)

	2	3	4	5
1	0	1	3	2
2	—	1	0	8
3	0	—	5	2
4	1	0	—	0

- $\beta_{5,1} = B_{Bnode} + \alpha(5, 1)$
= 30 + 0 (if any column and row not have any zero position then we will subtract smallest element from column that will treat as a α)
= 30 (Set distance (1, 5) as ∞)

	2	3	4	5
1	0	1	3	—
2	—	1	0	8
3	0	—	5	2
4	1	0	—	0

- Now again find set (P, Q) means find the location of zero element in matrix.

{(P, Q)} = {(1, 2) (2, 4) (3, 2) (4, 3) (4, 5)}
= {1, 4, 2, 1, 2} (The maximum of this L(*p*, *q*) is 4)

- A barred node $\overline{(2, 4)}$ is to be created to be created to the left of Bnode. Hence the lower bound for this barred node is:

30 + 4 = 34 (Now delete row 2 and column 4)

	2	3	5
1	0	1	—
3	0	—	2
4	1	0	0

- $\beta_{2,4} = B_{Bnode} + \alpha(2, 4)$

  $= 30 + 0$

  (if any column and row not have any zero position then we will subtract smallest element from column that will treat as a α)

  $= 30$ (Set distance (4, 2) as ∞)

	2	3	5
1	0	1	—
3	0	—	2
4	—	0	0

- Now again find set (P, Q) means find the location of zero element in matrix.

  {(P, Q)} = {(1, 2) (3, 2) (4, 3) (4, 5)}

  = {1, 2, 1, 2} (The maximum of this L(p, q) is 2)
- A barred node $\overline{(3, 2)}$ is to be created to the left of Bnode. Hence the lower bound for this barred node is:

  30 + 2 = 32 (Now delete row 3 and column 2)

	3	5
1	1	—
4	0	0

- $B_{3,2} = B_{Bnode} + \alpha(3, 2)$

  $= 30 + 1$

  (if any column not have any zero position then we will subtract smallest element from column that will treat as a α. Here 1st row not have any zero element so α will be 1)

  $= 31$

	3	5
1	0	—
4	0	0

- Now matrix is of dimension 2 × 2 then these are two links of diagonal element like (1, 3) (4, 5) which have zero position.

  {(5, 1) (2, 4) (3, 2) (1, 3) (4, 5)} *i.e.*, city should be visited as 5 – > 1 – > 3 – > 2 – > 4 – > 5

6.7 LONGEST COMMON SUBSEQUENCE

The **longest common substring problem** is to find the longest string that is a substring of two or more strings. The problem of longest common subsequence arises whenever we search for similarities across multiple texts. We can solve the problem of finding longest common subsequence by using Dynamic Programming. Start with a recursive algorithm for the problem, which may be inefficient because it calls itself repeatedly on a small number of sub-problems. Simply remember the solution to each sub-problem the first time you compute it, then after that look it up instead of re-computing it. The overall time bound then becomes (typically) proportional to the number of distinct sub-problems rather than the larger number of recursive calls. There are two ways of doing dynamic programming, top down and bottom-up. The top down (memorizing) method is closer to the original recursive algorithm, so easier to understand, but the bottom-up method is usually a little more efficient.

Why might we want to solve the longest common subsequence problem? There are several motivating applications.

- **Molecular biology:** DNA sequences (genes) can be represented as sequences of four letters ACGT, corresponding to the four sub-molecules forming DNA. When biologists find new sequences, they typically want to know what other sequences it is most similar to. One way of computing how similar two sequences are is to find the length of their longest common subsequence.
- **File comparison:** The Unix program "diff" is used to compare two different versions of the same file, to determine what changes have been made to the file. It works by finding a longest common subsequence of the lines of the two files; any line in the subsequence has not been changed, so what it displays is the remaining set of lines that have changed. In this instance of the problem we should think of each line of a file as being a single complicated character in a string.
- **Screen redisplay:** Many text editors like "emacs" display part of a file on the screen, updating the screen image as the file is changed. For slow dial-in terminals, these programs want to send the terminal as few characters as possible to cause it to update its display correctly. It is possible to view the computation of the minimum length sequence of characters needed to update the terminal as being a sort of common subsequence problem (the common subsequence tells you the parts of the display that are already correct and don't need to be changed).

Algorithm for LCS

```
LCS_length(X,Y)
m=length[X]
n=length[Y]
for i=1 to m
   do C[i,0]=0
for j=1 to n
```

```
    do C[0,j]=0
for i=1 to m
    do for j=1 to n
        do if xi=yi
        then C[i, j]=C[i-1, j-1]+1
            B [i,j]= ↖
        Else if C[i-1,j]>=C[i,j-1]
        Then C[i,j]=C[i-1,j]
            B[i,j]= ↑
        Else
            C[i,j]=C[i,j-1]
            B[i,j]= ←
        Return C,B
```

Algorithm to find subsequence

```
        Print LCS(b,x,i,j)
If i=0  or  j=0 then return
If b[i,j]= ↖
    Then Print LCS(b,x,i,j)
    Print xi
Else if b[i,j]= ↑
    Then Print LCS  (b,x,i-1,j)
    Else Print LCS  (b,x,i,j-1)
```

Example

		0	1	2	3	4
		yi	B	D	C	A
0	xi	0	0	0	0	0
1	A	0	0↑	0↑	0↑	1↖
2	B	0	1↖	1←	1←	1↑
3	C	0	1↑	1↑	2↖	2←
4	B	0	1↖	1↑	2 ↑	2↑

So the length of the longest common subsequence of sequences BDCA and ABCB is 2 and sequence is BC.

6.8 BACKTRACKING

The definition of backtracking in computer science is closely related to the brute-force search technique. Brute-force search is a general problem-solving technique that finds the solution trivially by systematically enumerating all of the possible candidates and then checking whether each of them meets the required criteria. Backtracking is a polished and smoother version of this.

Rather than just enlisting all of the possible candidates, backtracking enumerates just the really possible ones that already satisfy some of the properties of the problem; this can be built on to find the final answer moving forward. Therefore, it begins searching for the solution, and if it can't find anything going "one way" then it will "backtrack" and try another combination.

In the end it finds the final valid solution because, practically, it is going to try each possibility. In a nutshell, that's why it is called backtracking. The backtracking algorithms picks the first path and tries to go into its depth, searching for the solution; if it fails, then it steps backwards and picks the next path (another alternative), and so on.

In other words in the backtracking method, we need to solve the problem by systematic process until we get the solution. In the 3rd or 4th step if we find difficult to get the solution or there is no way to get the Solution means we need to move to the previous step and make changes over there to get a feasible solution in the next step this is called backtracking.

Terminology

Problem state is each node in the depth-first search tree.

State space is the set of all paths from root node to other nodes.

Solution states are the problem states *s* for which the path from the root node to *s* defines a tuple in the solution space.

- In variable tuple size formulation tree, all nodes are solution states.
- In fixed tuple size formulation tree, only the leaf nodes are solution states.
- Partitioned into disjoint sub-solution spaces at each internal node.

Answer states are that solution states *s* for which the path from root node to *s* defines a tuple that is a member of the set of solutions. These states satisfy implicit constraints.

State space tree is the tree organization of the solution space.

Static trees are ones for which tree organizations are independent of the problem instance being solved.

- Fixed tuple size formulation.
- Tree organization is independent of the problem instance being solved.

Dynamic trees are ones for which organization is dependent on problem instance.

Live node is a generated node for which all of the children have not been generated yet.

E-node is a live node whose children are currently being generated or explored.

Dead node is a generated node that is not to be expanded any further. All the children of a dead node are already generated.

Live nodes are killed using a **bounding function** to make them dead nodes.

6.8.1 N-Queen Problem

Before we begin, we need to phrase the "*Puzzle of N Queens.*" How can we place N queens on an N × N chessboard such that neither of them will attack each other? Of course, we know that such a placement is possible only when no two queens are to be found in the same row, column, or diagonal. Also, we won't stop right after the first solution. Our scope is to find all of the possible placements of those N queens on the board.

In this example we'll consider only a 4 × 4 board; thus, we have minimized our task to only 4 queens. As we discussed in the earlier section, we need to find a way to codify a series of candidates and ultimately the solution into vectors. In this case, it is pretty straightforward. There is no need to allocate the chessboard in its entirety (4 × 4 matrices) since we only need to know the positions of queens. We can do this only with a single-dimensional array (vector).

Consider the matrix

	C1	C2	C3	C4
R1				
R2				
R3				
R4				

Now place Q1 in row1/column1 so,

	C1	C2	C3	C4
R1				
R2				
R3				
R4				

Now Q2 should be placed in row2/column2, if we place in C2 × R2 the queens will be crossed because they are in the same diagonal. Therefore, the Q2 should be placed in C3 × R2

	C1	C2	C3	C4
R1				
R2				
R3				
R4				

Now place Q3 in row 3/column3, if we place in C3 × R3 the queens meet each other because they are in the same diagonal. Therefore, there is no solution the place the Q3 in the 3rd row/column.

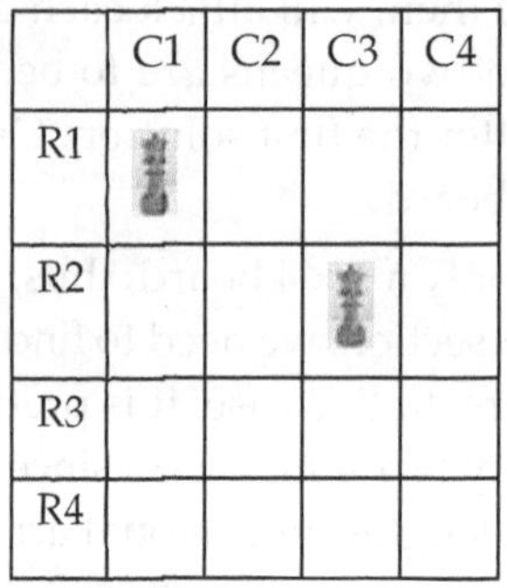

So, back track again, place the Q1 somewhere in the row, so move the Queen Q1 to C3 × R, and also move the position of Q2 so that these two queens should not affect the Q3. So place Q1 in R1 × C3 Place Q2 in R2 × C1

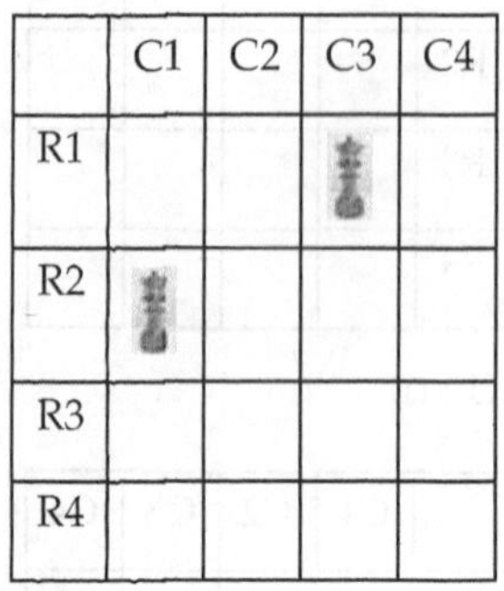

Now place Q3 in row 3/column 4. We cannot place in either R3 × C1 or R3 × C2 or R3 × C3 because the queens will meet each other. So place the queen in Q3 in R3 × C4.

Now place Q4 in row4/column 2. we cannot place Q4 in C1 or C3 or C4 so only solution is to place the Q4 in C2 × R4.

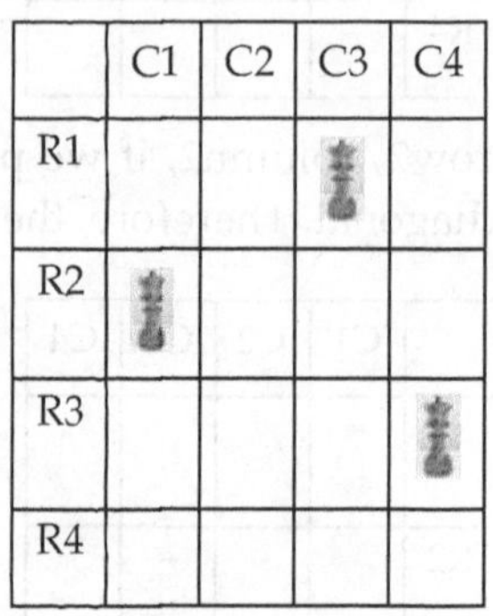

Now we got the solution in which we place the entire queen in 4x4 matrixes were in which no two queens meet each other.

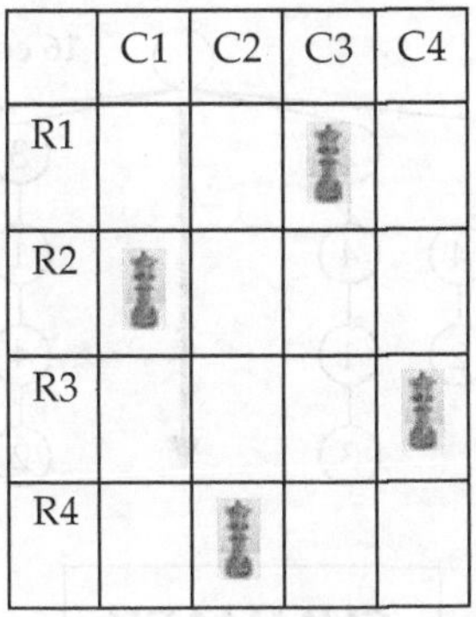

Algorithm Backtrack

```
function backtracking (current depth)
    if solution is valid
        return / print the solution
    else
        for each element from A [] source array
            let X[current depth] element
            if possible candidate (current depth + 1)
                backtracking (current depth + 1)
            end if
        end for
    end if
end function
```

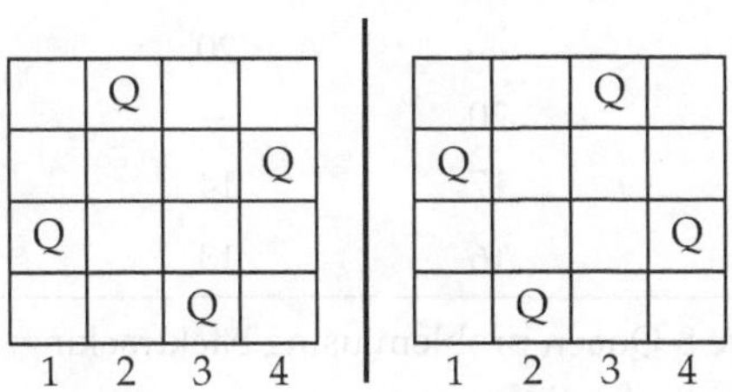

That's right. We have two possible placements in total. Remember what we said about the position of the queens? 2 4 1 3 means that X[1] = 2; X[2] = 4; X[3] = 1; X[4] = 3, meaning that first queen is located on (1,2), second on (2,4), third on (3,1), and the final fourth queen on (4,3).

If you want to see another visual example, check out the following diagram. In it you can see how the so-called "tree" is built if we approach backtracking from our tree analogy. Notice that the first node, the root node, is empty.

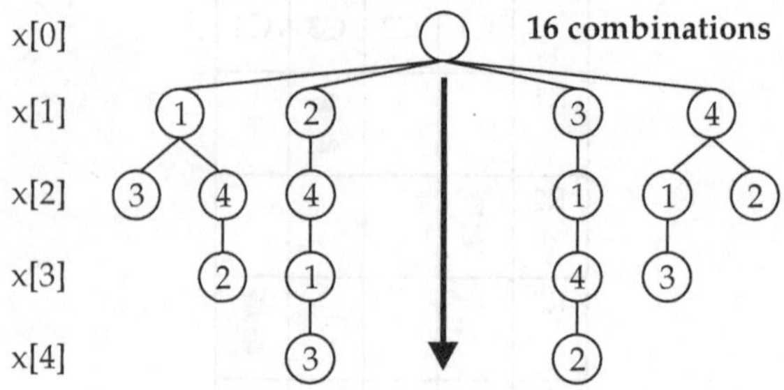

SUMMARY

Summing these up, backtracking ought to be used when no other algorithm or method is possible. By this I mean, it should be used in those cases when the problem can be reduced to some variation of the Descartes multiplication of some kind of arrays. Backtracking, due to its nature, isn't the most efficient technique; its run time can be quite high, and its complexity is just as bad. If any other alternative that gives a quicker result is possible, then it should be avoided. But when all of the results must be generated regardless, it does.

EXERCISE

1. Define dynamic programming. Give it's characteristics.
2. What is matrix chain multiplication problem? Solve the following problem:
   (*i*) *P*(6 × 5) Q(5 × 7) R(7 × 3) S (3 × 8) (*ii*) X(3 × 7) Y(7 × 4) Z(4 × 3)
3. What is TSP? Solve following problem using dynamic programming:

1	—	10	24	11	18
2	10	—	20	17	16
3	24	20	—	14	13
4	11	17	14	—	9
5	18	16	13	9	—

4. What is backtracking? Solve 8-Queen problem using backtracking.
5. Solve using matrix chain multiplication:
   A(4 × 10) B(10 × 3) C(3 × 12) D(12 × 20) E(20 × 7)

Hint:

	1	2	3	4	5
1	0	120,1	264,2,	1080,2	1344,2
2		0	360,2	1320,2	1350,2
3			0	720,3	1140,4
4				0	1680,4
5					0

Chapter 7 NP-COMPLETENESS

7.1 INTRODUCTION

Before we start: be reminded of our model of computation: all basic operations take unit time, we have infinite memory at the register level, and every step is determined deterministically as described in an algorithm. A polynomial algorithm is "faster" than an exponential algorithm. As n grows a^n always grows faster than n^k after certain integer n_0, for any integer values of a and k. Even 2^n grows faster than n^{1000} at some large value of n. The former functions are exponential and the later functions are polynomial. It seems that for some problems we just may not have any polynomial algorithm at all (as in the *information theoretic* bound)! The theory of NP-completeness is about this issue, and in general the computational complexity theory addresses it.

7.2 WHAT IS PROBLEM?

A **problem** is an obstacle, impediment, difficulty or challenge, or any situation that invites resolution; the resolution of which is recognized as a solution or contribution toward a known purpose or goal. A problem implies a desired outcome coupled with an apparent deficiency, doubt or inconsistency that prevents the outcome from taking place. Every theoretical problem asks for an answer or solution. Trying to find a solution to a problem is known as problem solving. That is, a problem is a gap between an actual and desired situation. The time it takes to solve a problem is a way of measuring complexity. Many problems have no discovered solution and are therefore classified as an open problem.

Example:

- Mathematical problem is a question about mathematical objects and structures that may require a distinct answer or explanation or proof. Examples include word problems at school level or deeper problems such as shading a map with only four colors.
- In society, a problem can refer to particular social issues, which if solved would yield social benefits, such as increased harmony or productivity, and conversely diminished hostility and disruption.

7.3 COMPUTATIONAL COMPLEXITY

Computational theory is concern with the study of intrinsic (essential nature of thing) complexity of computational task. It's final goal includes the determination of the complexity of any well defined task. The field of complexity theory deals with how fast can one solution of a certain type of problem can be found and more generally how much resources does it take viz time, memory space, number of processor etc. We can say fundamental area of theoretical computer science is complexity theory, the analysis of the resources needed to solve computational problems. Researchers in this area define computational models, such as Turing machines, Boolean Circuits, Parallel Random Access Machines, etc., and resource measures such as space, parallel time, amount of hardware, etc. A complexity class is then the set of problems solvable in a particular model under particular resource constraints. Models must be simple enough to allow mathematical analysis yet general enough to be useful in a wide context.

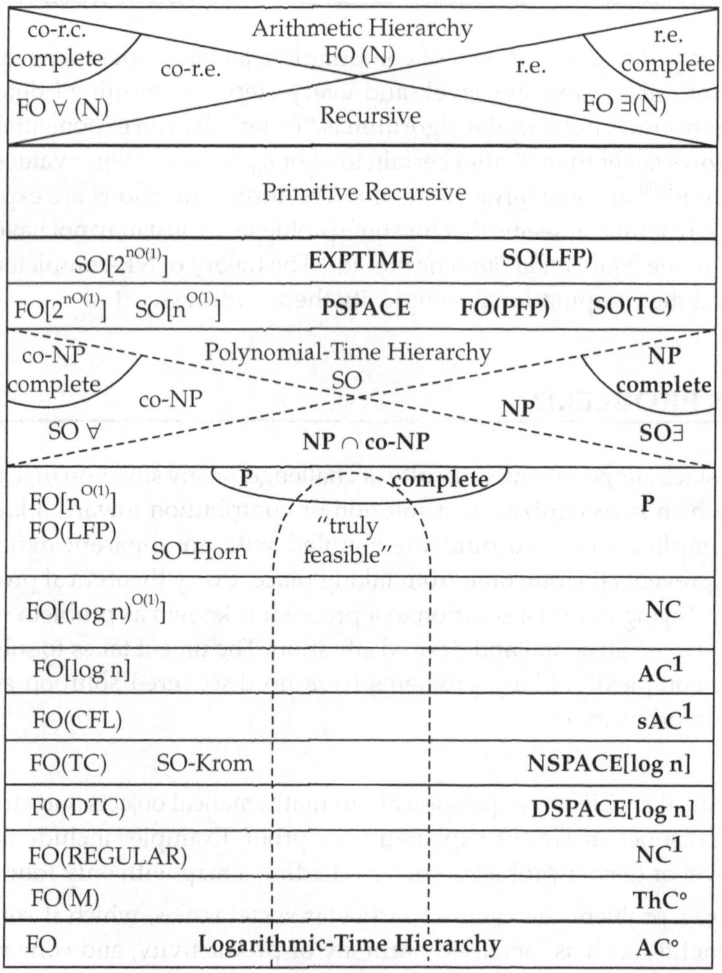

Perhaps the hardest thing to prove about a computational model is that it cannot solve a given problem within particular resource constraints. Such "lower bounds" are currently obtainable only when the model is very specialized or the constraints are very severe. The research project in Low-Level Complexity conducted by our group attempts to attack such problems by determining the relationships between complexity classes defined in various models by such very severe constraints.

Another project in complexity research studies the area called Descriptive Complexity. Computational complexity was originally defined in terms of the natural entities of time and space, and the term complexity was used to denote the time or space used in the computation. Rather than checking whether an input satisfies a property S, a more natural question might be, what is the complexity of expressing the property S? These two issues—checking and expressing—are closely related. It is startling how closely tied they are when the latter refers to expressing the property in first-order logic of finite and ordered structures. Here is a diagram of the world of computability and complexity.

Abstractly, a problem P is a set of pair (I, S), where I is an instance of the problem and S is a solution. We can categorize the problem basically in two parts: A **decision Problem** and an **Optimization Problem.**

Decision Problem: In computability theory and computational complexity theory, a decision problem is a question in some formal system with a yes-or-no answer, depending on the values of some input parameters. For example, the problem "given two numbers x and y, does x is greater by y?" is a decision problem. The answer can be either 'yes' or 'no', and depends upon the values of x and y.

Decision problems are closely related to function problems, which can have answers that are more complex than a simple 'yes' or 'no'. A corresponding function problem is "given two numbers x and y, what is x greater by y?" They are also related to optimization problems, which are concerned with finding the *best* answer to a particular problem.

A method for solving a decision problem given in the form of an algorithm is called a decision procedure for that problem. A decision procedure for the decision problem "given two numbers x and y, does x is greater by y?" would give the steps for determining whether x is greater by y, given x and y. One such algorithm is find maximum, taught to many school children. If subtraction is positive the answer produced is 'yes', otherwise it is 'no'. A decision problem which can be solved by an algorithm, such as this example, is called decidable.

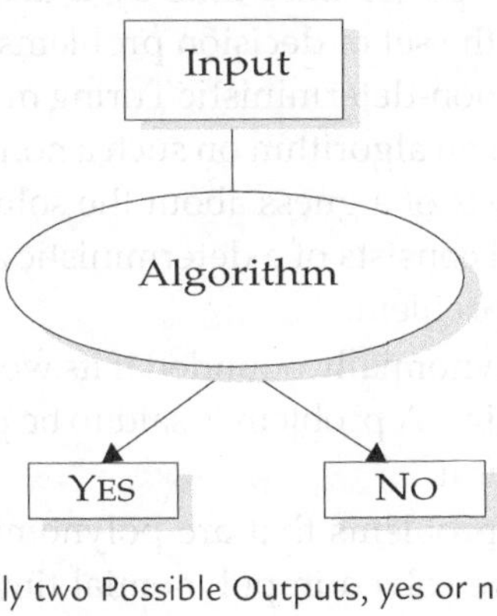

Fig. 7.1. A Decision Problem has only two Possible Outputs, yes or no (or alternately 1 or 0) on any Input

Optimization Problem: A computational problem in which the object is to find the best of all possible solutions. More formally, find a solution in the **feasible region** which has the minimum (or maximum) value of the **objective function**. An optimization problem O is a subset of a problem P, in which if (I, S) € O is a subset of a problem P, in which if (I, S) € O and (I, S′) € P then S ≤ S′ with respect to some ordering ≤ *i.e.* The solution S is better than S. In optimization problem asks, what is the best solution? A decision problem asks, is there a solution with a certain characteristic? For instance, the traveling salesman problem is an optimization problem, while the corresponding decision problem asks if there is a Hamiltonian cycle with a cost less than some fixed amount *k*.

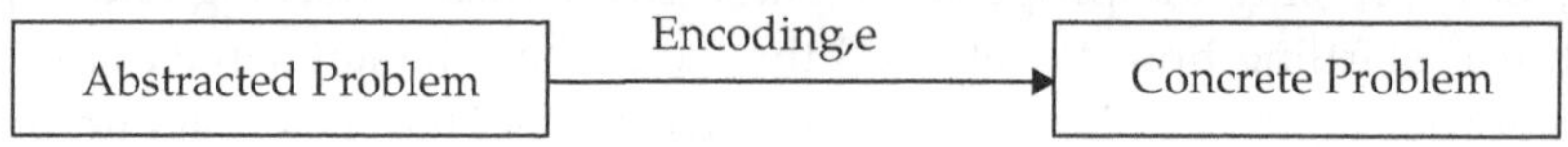

Example:

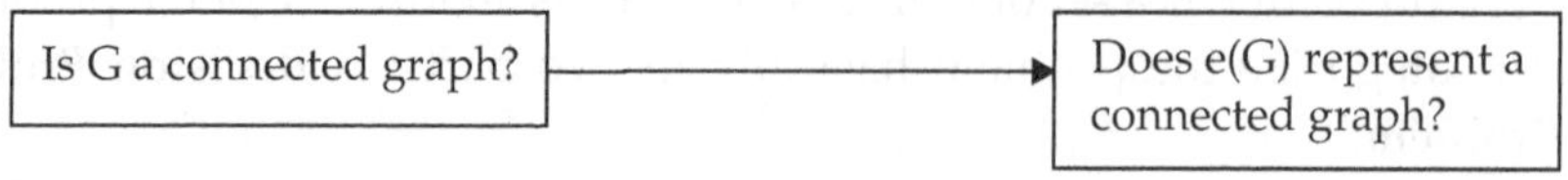

7.4 PROBLEM SOLVING

Problems can be classified on the basis of how much time they need to be solved. It means an algorithm solves a problem in time O(T(n)) if, for any instance I, the algorithm can produce a solution S in time O(T(1)).

Polynomial time solvable: A problem is assigned to the P (polynomial time) class if there exists at least one algorithm to solve that problem, such that the number of steps of the algorithm is bounded by a polynomial in n, where n is the length of the input.in other words a problem is polynomial time solvable if there is an algorithm to solve it in time O(n^k), for some constant k.

Non-Polynomial time solvable: In computational complexity theory, **NP** is one of the most fundamental complexity classes. The abbreviation **NP** refers to "non-deterministic polynomial time".Intuitively, **NP** is the set of all decision problems for which the instances where the answer is "yes" have efficiently verifiable proofs of the fact that the answer is indeed "yes". More precisely, these proofs have to be *verifiable* in polynomial time by a deterministic Turing machine. In an equivalent formal definition, **NP** is the set of decision problems where the "yes"-instances can be recognized in polynomial time by a non-deterministic Turing machine. The equivalence of the two definitions follows from the fact that an algorithm on such a non-deterministic machine consists of two phases, the first of which consists of a guess about the solution which is generated in a non-deterministic way, while the second consists of a deterministic algorithm which verifies or rejects the guess as a valid solution to the problem.

An algorithm is said to be polynomially bounded if its worst-case complexity is bounded by a polynomial function of the input size. A problem is said to be polynomially bounded if there is a polynomially bounded algorithm for it.

P is the class of all decision problems that are polynomially bounded. The implication is that a decision problem X € P can be solved in polynomial time on a deterministic computation model (such as a deterministic Turing machine).

NP represents the class of decision problems which can be solved in polynomial time by a non-deterministic model of computation. That is, a decision problem X € NP can be solved in polynomial-time on a non-deterministic computation model (such as a non-deterministic Turing machine). A non-deterministic model can make the right guesses on every move and race towards the solution much faster than a deterministic model.

A deterministic machine, at each point in time, executes an instruction. Depending on the outcome of executing the instruction, it then executes some next instruction, which is unique. A non-deterministic machine on the other hand has a choice of next steps. It is free to choose any that it wishes. For example, it can always choose a next step that leads to the best solution for the problem. A non-deterministic machine thus has the power of extremely good, optimal guessing.

As an example, let us consider the decision version of TSP: Given a complete, weighted graph and an integer k, does there exist a Hamiltonian cycle with total weight at most k?

A smart non-deterministic algorithm for the above problem starts with a vertex, guesses the correct edge to choose, proceeds to the next vertex, guesses the correct edge to choose there, etc. and in polynomial time discovers a Hamiltonian cycle of least cost and provides an answer to the above problem. This is the power of non-determinism. A deterministic algorithm here will have no choice but take super-polynomial time to answer the above question.

Another way of viewing the above is that given a candidate Hamiltonian cycle (call it certificate), one can verify in polynomial time whether the answer to the above question is YES or NO. Thus to check if a problem is in NP, it is enough to prove in polynomial time that any YES instance is correct. We do not have to worry about NO instances since the program always makes the right choice. So in short, we can define NP problems like:

Definition of NP: A decision problem Z is in the set NP if and only if there exists a Non Deterministic Turing Machine (NDTM) M that, when given an arbitrary instance x of Z on the input tape of M, will:

1. Non-deterministically place a string $w \in \Sigma^*$ on M's tape just to the left of instance x. If $x \in Y(Z)$, w will be the "answer" to instance x – that is, sufficient information, along with x, to verify (in step (2) below) that $x \in Y(Z)$. Otherwise, $x \in N(Z)$ and the string w will be a random set of characters, or empty (we need not verify instances in N(Z). If we can – fine, but it is not necessary); and

2. If $x \in Y(Z)$, deterministically (and in polynomial time with respect to $n = |x|$), verify that $x \in Y(Z)$, and finally halt in state q_Y. If $x \notin Y(Z)$ (*i.e.*, $x \in (N(Z))$), the machine M may halt in state q_N, or it may compute forever – we are only guaranteed that M will not halt in state q_Y.

It is easy to show that $P \subseteq NP$. However, it is unknown whether P = NP. In fact, this question is perhaps the most celebrated of all open problems in Computer Science.

7.5 REDUCTIONS

Suppose that, we have a decision problem A that we would like solve in polynomial time, suppose also that we have a second decision problem B for which we already have a polynomial-time algorithm for returning a verdict of "yes" or "no", then an algorithm for deciding problem A would exist if we had a polynomial-time algorithm for converting every instance of problem A into an instance of problem B and used the existing algorithm to decide that instance of B.

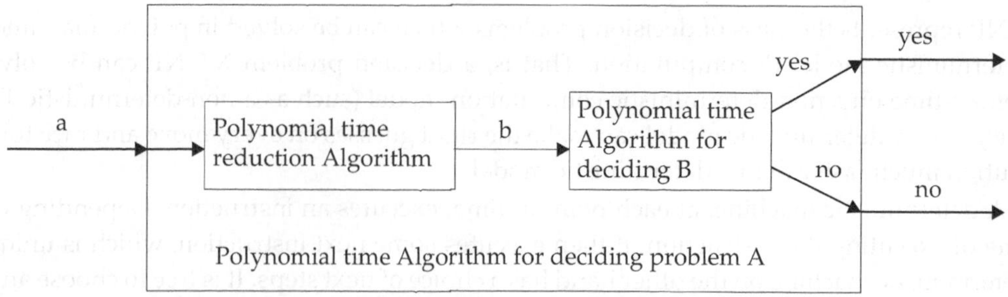

The procedure for converting instances A into instances of B is called a reduction, and it must have the following characteristics:

1. The transformation takes polynomial-time
2. The answers are the same—the answer to *a* is "yes" if and only if the answer to *b* is "yes".

The algorithm for deciding A in polynomial-time is illustrated in the figure above;

1. Use the polynomial-time algorithm to convert an instance a of problem A into an instance *b* of B
2. Run the polynomial-time algorithm to decide *b*
3. Use the decision for *b* as the answer for *a*

The two parts in sequence run in polynomial time, so the algorithm for deciding A will also be polynomial-time.

While it is neither necessarily common nor efficient to construct algorithms for solving problems in class **P** in this manner, such a construction is indeed feasible and will prove essential for constructing a subclass of **NP** called **NP-complete**. Finally all the NP problems are again categorize into two class **NP-Complete** and **NP-Hard.**

7.6 NP-COMPLETE

Generally this is a class of problems that are so difficult that even the best solutions cannot consistently determine their solutions in an efficient way. Specifically, NP Complete problems can only possibly be solved in polynomial time using a non-deterministic Turing machine (a computer capable of making guesses and checking them in polynomial time). Problems such as weather prediction, how to fill a box with odd-sized objects, and the Traveling Salesman problem fall into the realm of NP Complete problems. Because of the problem with finding the "best" solution, programs are often developed to find a usually reasonable solution.

NP-complete is a subset of NP, the set of all decision problems whose solutions can be verified in polynomial time; NP may be equivalently defined as the set of decision problems that can be solved in polynomial time on a non-deterministic Turing machine. A problem *p* in NP is also in NPC if and only if every other problem in NP can be transformed into *p* in polynomial time. NP-complete can also be used as an adjective: problems in the class NP-complete are known as NP-complete problems.

NP-complete problems are studied because the ability to quickly verify solutions to a problem (NP) seems to correlate with the ability to quickly solve that problem (P). It is not known whether every problem in NP can be quickly solved—this is called the P = NP problem. But, if *any single problem* in NP-complete can be solved quickly, then *every problem in NP* can also be quickly solved, because the definition of an NP-complete problem states that every problem in NP must be quickly reducible to every problem in NP-complete (that is, it can be reduced in polynomial time). Because of this, it is often said that the NP-complete problems are *harder* or *more difficult* than NP problems in general.

There are many equivalent ways of describing **NP**-completeness.

Let L be a language over a finite alphabet Σ.

L is **NP**-complete if, and only if, the following two conditions are satisfied:

1. L € NP; and
2. Any L′Ä NP is polynomial-time-reducible to L(written as $L' \le_p L$), where $L' \le_p L$ if, and only if, the following two conditions are satisfied:

(*i*) There exists $f : \Sigma^* \to \Sigma^*$ such that $\forall\, w \in \Sigma^*\ (w \in L' \Leftrightarrow f(w) \in L)$; and

(*ii*) There exists a polynomial-time Turing machine that halts with $f(w)$ on its tape on any input w

NP-Hard: NP-hard problems are usually optimization problems whose recognition version is NP-complete. For example the TSP-optimization is NP-hard because its TSP-recognition version is NP-complete (TSP-rec is as follows: given k is there a tour of length $\le k$?). Nemhauser and Wolsey say "A problem is NP-hard if there is an NP-complete problem that can be polynomially reduced to it." Thus, if a problem is NP-hard it is at least as difficult as any NP-complete problem.

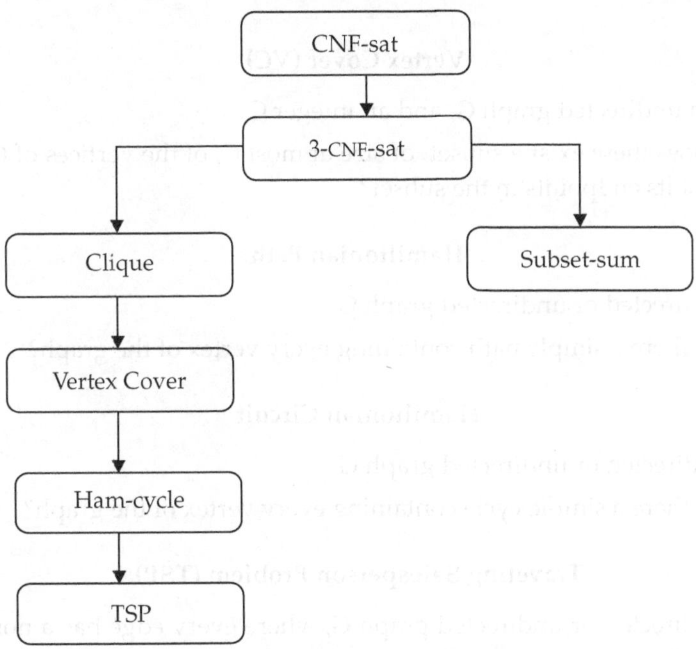

CNF Satisfiability

Instance: A set of n boolean variables and a conjunction of disjunctions of literals, where a literal is a variable or its negation.

Question: Is there a set of assignments of values to the variables that makes the conjunction true?

3 CNF Satisfiability
(3-CNF-SAT, or 3-SAT)

Instance: A set of n boolean variables and a conjunction of disjunctions of literals, where a literal is a variable or its negation, and each disjunction (clause) has exactly 3 literals.

Question: Is there a set of assignments of values to the variables that makes the conjunction true?

Subset Sum

Instance*:* A set S of items with integer weights, and an integer C

Question: Is there a subset X such that the total weight of the items in X is equal to C?

Clique

Instance: An undirected graph G, and an integer C

Question: Does there exist a complete subgraph of G of size at least C? That is, is there a subset of the vertices of G, of size at least C, such that every pair of vertices in the subset is connected by an edge?

Vertex Cover (VC)

Instance: An undirected graph G, and an integer C

Question: Does there exist a subset, of size at most C, of the vertices of G, such that every edge of G has one of its endpoints in the subset?

Hamiltonian Path

Instance: A directed or undirected graph G

Question: Is there a simple path containing every vertex of the graph?

Hamiltonian Circuit

Instance: A directed or undirected graph G

Question: Is there a simple cycle containing every vertex of the graph?

Traveling Salesperson Problem (TSP)

Instance: A directed or undirected graph G, where every edge has a nonnegative integer cost; and an integer C

Question: Is there a simple cycle containing every vertex of G, where the cycle cost (*i.e.*, the sum all its edge costs) is at most C?

7.7 COOK'S THEOREM

SAT is NP–Complete

For the following discussion Z is an arbitrary decision problem in NP, x is an arbitrary instance of Z (we assume valid instances of Z are polynomially recognizable by a DTM), and we assume the existence of a deterministic verifier M then, we will construct an instance of SAT that is true if and only if M, when given input x, results in M halting in state q_Y, that is, if and only if $x \in Y(Z)$.

The instance of SAT, $f(x)$, will be constructed prior to any computation by M. Therefore, every instance x maps to an instance of SAT. (Actually, both x and M are involved in the transformation, but M is the same for every instance x, so we can think of the transformation as being just a function of x.)

All instances of $x \in Y(Z)$ cause M to halt in state q_Y. Such instances will be mapped into satisfiable instances of SAT. All other instances will be mapped to SAT instances which can not be satisfied. That is, all instances $x \in Z$ which either cause M to halt in state q_N, or to loop forever. Now, we can claim:

1. $x \in Y(Z)$ if and only if M halts on x in state q_Y if and only if $f(x) \in Y(SAT)$; and
2. $x \in N(Z)$ if and only if M halts in state q_N or simply does not halt if and only if $f(x) \in N(SAT)$.

Note: We effectively ignore the complication that some instances in N(Z) might cause M to compute forever. Since they can not cause M to terminate in q_Y, we simply map them to instances in N(SAT). Therefore, if the construction of SAT, described next, is correct, SAT will be NP–Complete.

SAT Construction

To construct instances of SAT, we must define a set of Boolean variables and set of clauses that are consistent with our understanding of a given problem Z, an instance x, and a deterministic verifier M. The only properties we may assume are that Z is a decision problem in NP and, hence, has a polynomial time deterministic verifier M, and that x is a valid instance of Z. Therefore, with $n = |x|$, there is a polynomial $p(n)$ which bounds the computing time of M. It also places bounds on other aspects of M and the transformation. First, notice that the alphabet and M are fixed for problem Z. Therefore, their respective sizes are independent of the size of the instance x and, hence, are constants.

Alphabet: $\Sigma = \{s_0, s_1, \ldots, s_v\}$ where s_0 is a special "blank" character which does not appear in the language of Z. It is used only as a marker by M.

States of M: The states in M must include a start state q_0 and halt states q_1 and q_2 (for halt "yes" and halt "no"). Thus, we assume, for some constant $r \geq 3$, the states of M are $Q = \{q_0, q_1, \ldots, q_r\}$.

Tape cell contents and read/write head position: Initially, at time zero the tape contains the given instance $x = x_1x_2 \ldots x_n$ ($x_i \in \Sigma - \{s_0\}$) in "cells" 1, 2, …, n with the read/write head initially positioned on cell 1. Within $p(n)$ time (transitions), the head can never move more than $p(n)$ positions to the right, so we must have "blank's" in cells $n + 1, n + 2, \ldots, p(n) + 1$. Cells to the left of position 1 (*i.e.*, cell 0, –1, –2, …, $-p(n)$) are filled by the nondeterministic "answer," but will not exceed that needed by $p(n)$ possible moves to the left. So, we need only keep track of tape cell contents, and the position of the read/write head, for cells $-p(n), -p(n) + 1, \ldots, p(n) + 1$. Notice, this also implies the non deterministic answer for a yes instance can not be exponentially large.

Now we introduce a set of Boolean variables whose assignments corresponds to whether or not M, when given string x, is at time i in state j, the tape head positioned at tape cell k, and tape cell k contains character c, for all times i, states j, tape cell positions k, and characters c.

Variables

At time i, for $0 \le i \le p(n)$,

$Q[i, k]$	$0 \le k \le r$	M is in state q_k.
$H[i, j]$	$-p(n) \le j \le p(n)+1$	The r/w head is on cell j.
$S[i, j, k]$	$-p(n) \le j \le p(n) + 1; 0 \le k \le n$	The contents of cell j is s_k.

This gives an order of $4p^2(n)$ variables, *i.e.*, a polynomial number of variables with respect to $n = |x|$. Intuitively, we will now construct clauses in such a way that allows (forces) these variables to have a satisfiable assignment consistent with M reading x and finally terminating in state q_1 if and only if $x \in Y(Z)$. For example, if $x \in Y(Z)$, M must be in the start state at time 0 and in state q_1 at time $p(n)$. So, we could have clauses $\{Q[0, 0]\}$ and $\{Q[p(n), 1]\}$. In fact, we will. We could also have a collection of clauses $\{\neg Q[0,k]\}$ for $0 < k \le p(n)$, since M cannot be in any of the other states at time 0. In fact, we will not, because there will be another set of clauses that will subsume this set. But, this is the general idea, clauses will enforce a correspondence that can be satisfied if and only if they reflect the "physical" properties of a "properly running" Deterministic Turing Machine.

Other clauses will be produced which can be satisfied if and only if there is a sequence of state transitions, head movements, and tape contents that lead M to state q_1, a property of M when given $x \in Y(Z)$. These clauses cannot be satisfied for any instance in N(Z) since M cannot then enter state q_1.

Conclusions

Since SAT is NP–Complete, 3–Sat is NP–Complete. This, in turn, implies Vertex Cover is NP–Complete. Hence, Independent Set and Clique are both NP–Complete. We also can conclude that

1. If any problem Z in NP–Complete can be solved in polynomial time be a DTM, then all problems in NP can be solved in deterministic polynomial time, *i.e.*, P = NP, and
2. If any problem Z in NP–Complete requires an exponential time DTM, then all problems in NP–Complete require an exponential time DTM, *i.e.*, P ≠ NP.

SUMMARY

P, NP, NP-Complete and NP-Hard are sets of problems, defined as follows:

- **P:** problems whose solution is polynomial time in the size of their inputs.
- **NP:** problems whose solutions can be verified in polynomial time. (NP stands for *non-deterministic polynomial time*).
- **NP-Complete:** A collection of problems in NP whose solutions may or may not polynomial time. We don't know. However, if we can prove that one of them may be solved in polynomial time, then all of them can.

- **NP-Hard:** A collection of problems that are not in NP, whose solutions are at least as hard as the NP-Complete problems.

  In this lecture, we learned that what it takes to prove that problems belong to these sets. Suppose we have a problem to solve, and we want to know its complexity class. This takes two steps:

1. *Prove that it is in NP*. Typically the problem is couched as a **yes** or **no** problem involving a data structure, such as "does there exist a simple cycle through a given directed graph that visits all the nodes?" To prove it is in NP, we need to show that a **yes** solution can be checked in polynomial time. In the above example, we can check to see if a given path through the graph is indeed a simple cycle in linear time. Therefore, the problem is in **NP**. We don't have to prove anything about the **no** solutions, and we don't have to prove anything about how we'd calculate a solution.
2. *Transform a known NP. Complete problem to this one in polynomial time*. Suppose the problem in question is **Q**, and that **L** is a well-known NP-Complete problem like the *3-satisfiability* problem. We need to show that if we have any instance of problem **L**, we can transform it into an instance of problem **Q** in polynomial time. Thus, if we could solve problem **Q** in polynomial time, we could solve problem **L** in polynomial time.

If we can do both of these things, then we have proved that a problem is NP-Complete. If we can prove that either of these things cannot be done, then we have proved that a problem is not NP-Complete. Sometimes we can't do come up with good proofs, and we just don't know.

The complexity classes P and NP-Hard may be put in terms of the above:

- **P:** If we can prove that the solution to a problem may be calculated in polynomial time, then the problem is in P. All of the algorithms that we have studied in this class are in **P**.
- **NP-Hard:** These are problems that are not in NP; however, we can perform the transformation in step 2 of a known NP-Complete problem to these problems. Thus, they are *at least as hard* as the NP-Complete problems.

EXERCISE

1. Briefly explain NP-Hard and NP-Completeness with examples.
2. When a decision problem is said to be polynomially reducible?
3. Explain NP-complete problems.
4. Explain the halting problem.
5. Explain undecidable problems.
6. Explain class P problems.
7. Explain the theory of computational complexity.
8. Define tractable and intractable problems.
9. What is Clique Decision Problem? Show that clique optimization reduces to clique decision problem.
10. What do you mean by deterministic and Non Deterministic Algorithms? Differentiate between them. Write example for each of them.
11. State the properties of NP hard problem.

APPENDIX

- Algorithm
- Finiteness
- Definiteness
- Deterministic
- Natural Language
- Pseudo-code
- FlowChart algorithm
- Dynamic Programming
- Greedy algorithm
- Brute force algorithm
- Randomized algorithm
- Branch and bound algorithm
- Recursive algorithm
- Back tracking algorithm
- Divide and conquer algorithm
- Recurring
- Serial algorithm
- Parallel algorithm
- Priory analysis
- Posteriori analysis
- Design phase
- Time complexity
- Input classes
- Space complexity
- Program space
- Instruction space
- Environment Stack space
- Data space
- Operation count
- Step count
- Frequency count
- Model of computation
- Random access machine
- Finite automaton
- Turing machine
- Problem size
- Worst case analysis
- Average case analysis
- Best case analysis
- Growth order
- Growth rate
- Asymptotic complexity
- Asymptotic notation
- Running time
- Big oh notation
- Big omega notation
- Theta notation
- Little oh notation
- Little omega
- Exponential function
- Data structure
- List
- Ordered list
- Set
- Multi set
- Double ended Queue (Dequeue)
- Stack
- Queue

- Linked list
- Tree
- Graph
- Array
- Doubly linked list
- Circular list
- Binary tree
- Abstract view
- Abstract data type (ADT)
- Interface
- LIFO
- Push
- Pop
- Dup
- Swap
- Rotate
- IsEmpty
- Stack Pointer
- IsFull
- Initialize
- Destroy
- Postponement
- Prefix
- Infix
- Postfix
- Backtracking
- FIFO
- Front
- Rear
- Enqueue
- Top
- Priority queue
- Tree
  - *Parent node*
  - *Child node*
  - *Leaf node*
  - *Terminal node*
  - *Height*
  - *Depth*
  - *Root node*
  - *Internal node*
  - *Inner node*
  - *Subtree*
  - *Proper subtree*
  - *Forest*
  - Weighted graph
  - Path
  - Cycle
  - Indegree
  - Outdegree
  - Connected graph
- Adjacency matrix
- Adjacency list
- Graph traversal
- BFS (breadth first search)
- DFS (depth first search)
- Conquer
- Memory access
- Parallelism
- Subroutine
- Partition phase
- Sort phase
- Pivot
- Strassen's matrix
- Multiplication
- Recurrence relation
- Iteration method
- Feasible solution
- Objective function
- Optimal solution
- Candidate set
- Selection function
- Feasibility function
- Solution function
- Greedy choice property
- Optimal substructure
- Minimum spanning tree
- Kruskal's algorithm
- Prim's algorithm

Fractional knapsack
Shortest path
Rucksack problem
Single source shortest path
Negative cost cycle
Branch and bound
Branching
Bounding
Pruning
Live node
E node
Dead note
List cost search
Combinatorial optimization problem
Cost function
01 knapsack
Traveling salesman problem
Top down
Bottom up
Principle of optimality
Matrix and multiplication
Symmetric traveling salesman problem
B node
Barred node
Longest common subsequence
Back tracking
Problem state
State space
Solution state
Answer state
State space tree
Static tree
Dynamic tree
N queen problem
4 queen problem
8 queen problem
Polynomial time
Non-polynomial time
Reduction
Satisfiability
NP
P
NP-Hard
NP-Complete
SAT
Vertex Cover
Hamilton Cycle
Turing Machine
Non-deterministic Turing Machine

Bibliography

- Aho, Alfred V., *"Data structures and algorithms"*, Reading, Mass: Addison-Wesley, c1983.
- Aho, Alfred V., *"The design and analysis of computer algorithm"*.
- Edited by Attallah, Mikhail J. *"Algorithms and theory of computation handbook"*, CRC Press, 1998 (QA76.9.A43 1999).
- Baase, Sara., *"Computer algorithms: introduction to design and analysis"*, Reading, Mass: Addison-Wesley Pub. Co., c1978.
- Brassard, Giles. and Bratley, Paul. *"Algoritmics: Theory and Practice"*, (QA9.6 .B73 1988).
- Brassard, Gilles, *"Fundamentals of algorithmics"*, Englewood, N.J.: Prentice Hall, c1996.
- Brown, Marc H. *"Algorithm animation"*, Cambridge, Mass: M.I.T. Press, c1988.
- Budd, Timothy A., *"Classic data structures in C++ Reading"*, Mass.: Addison-Wesley Pub. Co., c1994.
- Collected algorithms from ACM. New York, N.Y: Association for Computing Machinery, 1975-. (MICROFICHE)
- Cormen, Thomas H. *"Introduction to algorithms"*, Cambridge, Mass: MIT Press ; New York: McGraw-Hill, c1990.
- Even, Shimon., *"Graph Algorithms"*,Computer Science Press, 1979.
- Garey, Michael R., *"Computers and intractability: a guide to the theory of NP"*, San Francisco: W. H. Freeman, c1979.
- Gibbons, Alan M., *"Efficient Parallel Algorithms"*, Cambridge University Press, 1988.
- Greene, Daniel H., *"Mathematics for the analysis of algorithms"*, Boston: Birkhauser, c1981.
- Gonnet, Gaston H., *"Handbook of algorithms and data structures: in Pascal and C"*, Wokingham, England ; Reading, Mass: Addison-Wesley Pub. Co.,
- Gonnet, Gaston H. and Baeza-Yates, Ricardo editors, *"Handbook of Algorithms and Data Structures in Pascal and C"*, Addison-Wesley, 1991.
- Grossman, Jerrold W., *"Discrete Mathematics: An Introduction to Concepts, Methods, and Applications"*, (Macmillan/Prentice-Hall, 1990)
- Harel, David., *"Algorithmics: the spirit of computing"*, second edition Addison-Wesley, 1992.
- Horowitz, Ellis., *"Fundamentals of computer algorithms"*, Potomac, Md: Computer Science Press, c1978.

- Smith, Jeffrey D., *"Design and Analysis of Algorithms"*, PWS-Kent, 1989.
- Kingston, Jeffrey Howard., *"Algorithms and data structures*: design, correctness, analysis", Sydney: Addison-Wesley, 1990.
- Koren, Israel., *"Computer Arithmetic Algorithms"*, Prentice-Hall, 1993.
- Kozen, Dexter C. *"The design and analysis of algorithms"*, 1992.(QA76.9.A43 K69 1992).
- Kreher, Donald L. and Stinson, Douglas Combinatorial Algorithms: Generation, Enumeration and Search, (CRC Press, 1998)
- Kruse, Robert L., *"Data Structures and Program Design"*, second edition Prentice-Hall, 1996.
- Knuth, Donald E,. Graham, Ronald L. and Patashnik, Oren.,*"Concrete Mathematics: A Foundation for Computer Science"*, second edition Wiley, 1990.
- Leighton, F. Thomson.,*"Introduction to Parallel Algorithms and Architectures: Arrays, Trees, Hypercubes"*, Morgan Kaufman, 1992.
- Machtey, Michael., *"An introduction to the general theory of algorithms"*, New York: North Holland, c1978.
- Manber, Udi., *"Introduction to Algorithms"*, Addison-Wesley, 1989.
- Mehlhorn, Kurt, *"UNIF Effiziente Allgorithmen. English. Data structures and algorithms"*, Berlin ; New York: Springer, 1984. 1984 DAT V. 2, 1984 DAT V. 3, 1984 DAT V. 1.
- Moffat, David V., *"Common algorithms in Pascal with programs for reading"*, Englewood Cliffs, N.J: Prentice-Hall, c1984.
- Moret, B. M. E. (Bernard M. E.), *"Algorithms from P to NP"*, Redwood City, CA: Benjamin/ Cummings, c1991.
- Reinelt, G. (Gerhard),*"The traveling salesman: computational solutions for TSP"*, Berlin; New York: Springer-Verlag, c1994.
- Reingold, Edward M., Nievergelt, Jurg. and Deo, Narsingh., *"Combinatorial Algorithms: Theory and Practice"*, Prentice-Hall, 1977.
- Rosen, Kenneth H.,*" Discrete Mathematics and Its Applications"*, McGraw-Hill, 1999.
- Sedgewick, Robert, *"Algorithms"* Reading, Mass: Addison-Wesley, c1983.
- Sedgewick, Robert, *"Algorithms in C"*, Reading, Mass: Addison-Wesley Pub. Co., c1990.
- Skiena, Steven S. *"The Algorithm Design Manual"*. with CD-ROM.
- Standish, Thomas A., *"Data Structures, Algorithms, and Software Principles"*, Addison-Wesley, 1994.
- Standish, Thomas A., *"Data structure techniques Reading"*, MA: Addison-Wesley, c1980.
- Tremblay, Jean-Paul., *"An Introduction to computer science: an algorithmic approach"*, New York: McGraw-Hill, c1979.
- Walker, Henry M.,*"Computer science 2: principles of software engineering, data"*, Glenview, Ill: Scott, Foresman, c1989.
- Wirth, Niklaus., *"Algorithms + data structures=programs"*, Englewood Cliffs, N.J: Prentice-Hall, c1976.

- Thomas H. Cormen, Charles E. Leiserson, and Ronald L. Rivest, *Introduction to Algorithms* (MIT Press, 2000).
- Brassard, G. and Bratley, P. Fundamental of Algorithmics, Prentice-Hall, 1996.
- Anany V. Levitin, *Introduction to the Design and Analysis of Algorithms* (Addison Wesley, 2002).
- a b c Donald E. Knuth, *The Art of Computer Programming: Volume 3, Sorting and Searching*, second edition (Addison-Wesley, 1998).
- Heideman, M. T., D. H. Johnson, and C. S. Burrus, "Gauss and the history of the fast Fourier transform," IEEE ASSP Magazine, 1, (4), 14–21 (1984)
- Knuth, Donald (1998). *The Art of Computer Programming: Volume 3 Sorting and Searching*. pp. 159. ISBN 0-201-89685-0.
- Karatsuba, Anatolii A.; Yuri P. Ofman (1962). "У множение многозмачных чисеπ на aBTOMaTax". *Doklady Akademii Nauk SSSR* 146: 293–294. Translated in *Physics-Doklady* **7**: 595–596. 1963.
- M. Frigo; C. E. Leiserson, H. Prokop (1999). *"Cache-oblivious algorithms"*. *Proc. 40th Symp. On the Foundations of Computer Science.*
- Nicholas J. Higham, *"The accuracy of floating point summation"*, *SIAM J. Scientific Computing* **14** (4), 783–799 (1993).
- Thomas H. Cormen, Charles E. Leiserson, Ronald L. Rivest, and Clifford Stein. *Introduction to Algorithms*, Second Edition. MIT Press and McGraw-Hill, 2001. ISBN 0-262-03293-7. Chapter 28: Section 28.2: Strassen's algorithm for matrix multiplication, pp.735–741.
- *Introduction to Algorithms* (Cormen, Leiserson, and Rivest) 1990, Chapter 16 *"Greedy Algorithms"* p. 329.
- *Introduction to Algorithms* (Cormen, Leiserson, Rivest, and Stein) 2001, Chapter 16 *"Greedy Algorithms"*.
- V. Jarník: *O jistém problému minimálním* [About a certain minimal problem], Práce Moravské Pørodov ìdecké Spoleènosti, 6, 1930, pp. 57-63. (in Czech)
- R. C. Prim: *Shortest connection networks and some generalisations*. In: *Bell System Technical Journal*, 36 (1957), pp. 1389–1401
- D. Cherition and R. E. Tarjan: *Finding minimum spanning trees*. In: *SIAM Journal of Computing*, 5 (Dec. 1976), pp. 724–741
- Thomas H. Cormen, Charles E. Leiserson, Ronald L. Rivest, and Clifford Stein. *Introduction to Algorithms*, Second Edition. MIT Press and McGraw-Hill, 2001. ISBN 0-262-03293-7. Section 23.2: The algorithms of Kruskal and Prim, pp.567–574.
- Garey, Michael R.; David S. Johnson (1979). *Computers and Intractability: A Guide to the Theory of NP-Completeness*. W.H. Freeman. ISBN 0-7167-1045-5. A6: MP9, pg.247.
- Silvano Martello; Paolo Toth (1990). *Knapsack Problems: Algorithms and Computer Implementations*. John Wiley & Sons. ISBN 0-471-92420-2.
- Kellerer, Hans; U. Pferschy, D. Pisinger (2005). *Knapsack Problems*. Springer Verlag. ISBN 3-540-40286-1.

- Thomas H. Cormen, Charles E. Leiserson, Ronald L. Rivest, and Clifford Stein. *Introduction to Algorithms*, Second Edition. MIT Press and McGraw-Hill, 1990. ISBN 0-262-03293-7. Chapter 4: Recurrences, pp. 62–90.
- Thomas H. Cormen, Charles E. Leiserson, Ronald L. Rivest, and Clifford Stein, ed (2001). *"Single-Source Shortest Paths". Introduction to Algorithms* (2nd ed.). Cambridge, Massachusetts: MIT Press. pp. 580–642. ISBN 978-0-262-03293-3. OCLC 46792720.
- E. W. Dijkstra: *A note on two problems in connexion with graphs*. In *Numerische Mathematik*, 1 (1959), S. 269–271.
- Thomas H. Cormen, Charles E. Leiserson, Ronald L. Rivest, and Clifford Stein. *Introduction to Algorithms*, Second Edition. MIT Press and McGraw-Hill, 2001. ISBN 0-262-03293-7. Section 24.3: Dijkstra's algorithm, pp.595–601
- *http://www.devarticles.com/c/a/Development-Cycles/*
- *http://www.devarticles.com/c/a/Development-Cycles/Branch-and-Bound-Algorithm-Technique/3/*
- *http://www.academic.marist.edu/~jzbv/algorithms/Branch%20and%20Bound.htm*
- *www.cs.umsl.edu/~sanjiv/classes/cs5130/lectures/bb.pdf*
- *www.cs.sandia.gov/opt/survey/branch-and-bound.html*
- *http://en.wikipedia.org/wiki/*
- *http://net.pku.edu.cn/~course/cs101/resource/Intro2Algorithm/book6/chap11.htm*
- *www.dcs.vein.hu/CIR/cikkek/Elementary_Data_Structures.pdf*
- *www.undergraduate.csse.uwa.edu.au/units/CITS1005/lectures/topic16.pdf*
- *www.csse.monash.edu.au/~lloyd/tildeAlgDS/*
- *www.sc.isc.tohoku.ac.jp/class/algorithm2002/100402-nakag.pdf*
- *www.net.pku.edu.cn/~course/cs101/resource/.../chap11.htm*
- *www.curry.ateneo.net/~jpv/DS/DSJul04/ElemDS.ppt*
- *www.cs.duke.edu/~reif/courses/alglectures/skiena.../lecture7.pdf*
- *www.en.wikipedia.org/wiki/Divide_and_conquer_algorithm*
- *www.cs.berkeley.edu/~vazirani/algorithms/chap2.pdf -*
- *www.csc.liv.ac.uk/~ped/teachadmin/algor/d_and_c.html*
- *www.divideandconquer.se/*
- *www.en.wikipedia.org/wiki/**Travelling_salesman_problem***
- *www.**tsp**.gatech.edu/*
- *www.lalena.com/AI/**Tsp**/*
- *www.patol.com/java/**TSP**/*
- *www.hermetic.ch/misc/ts3/ts3demo.htm*
- *http://.en.wikipedia.org/.../**Longest_common_subsequence**_problem*
- *www.wordaligned.org/articles/**longest-common-subsequence***

- *www.ics.uci.edu*
- *www.algorithmist.com/index.../**Longest_Common_Subsequence***
- *www.durangobill.com/**N_Queens**.html*
- *www.animatedrecursion.com/.../the_eight_**queens_problem**.html*
- *www.bridges.canterbury.ac.nz/features/eight.html*
- *http://www.cs.umass.edu/~immerman/complexity_theory.html*
- *http://en.wikipedia.org/wiki/NP_%28complexity%29*
- *http://www.lcm.csa.iisc.ernet.in/dsa/node226.html*

QUESTION BANK

1. What is Algorithm?
2. What is the tool for analyzing the time efficiency of a non-recursive Algorithm?
3. What are the three ways by which an algorithm can be analyzed?
4. How the mathematical analysis can be performed?
5. What are the two categories of algorithms?
6. Write an algorithm for a given numbers n to generate the nth number of the Fibonacci sequence.
7. Find the number of comparisons made by the sequential search in the worst and Best case.
8. Write any four examples for Brute Force Approach.
9. Find the number of comparisons made by the sequential search in the worst and Best case.
10. Give the time efficiency and Drawback of merge sort algorithm.
11. What is the difference between DFS and BFS?
12. What is the Brute Force Algorithmic Strategy?
13. State the time complexity of following:
    (*i*) Bubble sort (*ii*) Selection sort (*iii*) Sequential search
14. Define "Divide and Conquer Technique".
15. Define Merge sort and explain three steps of Merge sort.
16. Define Quick sort and explain three steps of Quick sort.
17. Define Binary Search.
18. What are the applications of binary search?
19. State advantages and Disadvantages of binary search.
20. Explain Binary search tree.
21. What is the recurrence relation for divide and conquer?
22. Write any four advantages of insertion sort.
23. What are the two types of searching algorithm?
24. How efficient is prim's algorithm?

25. State the following terms:

    (*i*) Balanced Tree (*ii*) Unbalanced Tree
26. What is height of balanced tree?
27. What are the drawbacks of AVL trees?
28. Define Heap and what are the two types heap?
29. What are the important properties of heap?
30. Define complete binary tree.
31. What is the height of the tree? (or) depth of the tree?
32. Define almost complete binary tree.
33. What are the features of heap sort?
34. Define heapsort.
35. State the properties of AVL trees.
36. What is Greedy method?
37. Define Prim's algorithm.
38. Define Kruskal's algorithm.
39. Define Dijikstra's shortest path algorithm.
40. What are the applications of spanning trees?
41. Define Branch and Bound method.
42. Define Knapsack's problem.
43. Define Travelling salesman problem.
44. What are the applications of branch and bound?
45. Solve the following instance of the knapsack problem by the branch and bound algorithm.
46. Discuss the solution for Travelling salesman problem using branch and bound technique.
47. What is dynamic programming?
48. Compare divide and conquer and Dynamic programming.
49. How the problems can be solved using dynamic programming?
50. Give any two properties of dynamic programming approach.
51. Define principle of optimality.
52. Compare Greedy algorithm and Dynamic programming.
53. Construct a minimum spanning tree using Kruskal's algorithm with your own example.
54. Solve the all pair shortest path problem for the diagraph with the weighted matrix given below:

a	*b*	*c*	*d*	
a	0	∞	3	∞
b	2	0	∞	∞

c	∞	7	0	1
d	6	∞	∞	0

55. Define Spanning tree. Discuss design steps in Prim's algorithm to construct minimum spanning tree with an example.
56. Explain Dijikstra algorithm.
57. Define Backtracking.
58. What are the applications of backtracking?
59. What are the algorithm design techniques?
60. Define *n*-queens problem.
61. What is state space tree?
62. State principle of backtracking.
63. Compare Backtracking and Branch and Bound techniques with an example.
64. What are the examples of branch and bound?
65. Obtain all possible solutions to 4-Queen's problem.
66. Generate atleast 3-solutions for 5-Queen's problem.
67. Explain the *n*-Queen's problem and discuss the possible solutions.
68. Design an algorithm for checking whether the given word is a palindrome.
69. What is algorithm visualization?
70. Write the pseudo code for greedy method.
71. State the basic principle of divide and conquer strategy with the pseudocode.
72. State TSP.
73. State multistage graph problem give an application of this problem.
74. What is meant by branch and bound tech?
75. Write down the adjacency matrix of the following graph (refer graph from paper).
76. Define articulation point and biconnected component with example.
77. State the properties of NP hard problem.
78. Differentiate between Binary and Binary Search Tree.
79. What is the worst case running time of Quick Sort?
80. What is the worst case running time of algorithm to delete each element from the linked list?
81. Which is more efficient of BFS and DFS?
82. What are maximum and minimum number of elements in a heap of height *h*?
83. Where in a heap might the smallest element reside?
84. Differentiate between NP Hard and NP Complete .
85. What is time complexity ?
86. What is space complexity?

87. Give brief concept of Divide and conquer.
88. Write an algorithm to sort an array containing 0's and 1's with complexity of order of n .
89. What is recursion? What are its drawbacks?
90. The order of complexity of Binary Search in Best case is _____ in the average case is _____ in the Worst case is _____.
91. If W = MNOP, list all substrings of W.
92. Define the term Divide and Conquer.
93. How does heap Sort work?
94. Explain the backtracking Problem with 4 Queens on a 4*4 chess board.
95. Define non deterministic algorithm.
96. Write an algorithm that will traverse a binary tree level by level. That is root is visited first then.
97. The intermediate children of root then grand children of root and so on.
98. What are the advantages of dynamic programming over greedy method?
99. What are the various techniques for design of various algorithms?
100. How the time and space complexities measured for an algorithm?
101. What is the order of Bubble Sort?
102. What are the conditions under which backtracking can be used?
103. What is Optimal Merge Pattern Problem?
104. What is algorithm for in order traversal?
105. What is solution space in Backtracking Techniques ?
106. How will Merge Sort sort the 6 numbers:
107. 40, 10, 20 , 18, 16, 62 by divide and conquer technique.
108. What is Binary Search Tree?
109. What are various steps used in design of an algorithms? Give an example of algorithm which is Infinite in nature.
110. What is the order of the computation for the following loop:

     For ($i = 1, i < n, i + 1$)

     For ($j = 1, j < n, j + 1$)
111. Give the definition for 0/1 knapsack problem.
112. What are the various set operations possible?
113. What is algorithm of Pre Order Traversal.
114. What is NP Hard Problem?
115. What is Ordering Paradigm?
116. Differentiate between full and complete Binary Tree.
117. Write an algorithm for insertion sort. Also give its computing time.

118. What is lower bound?
119. What are explicit and implicit constraints?
120. What is algebraic simplification?
121. How will *u* represent a polynomial using dense representation strategy.
122. Differentiate between Deterministic and Non-deterministic algorithms.
123. What is Criterion Function?
124. Define the Principal of Optimality.
125. What are Decision Problems?
126. What is Interpolation of polynomial?
127. Describe an algorithm to insert and delete edges in the adjacency list representation for an undirected graph. Remember that the edge (i, j) appears on the adjacency list for both vertex i and j.
128. Give an algorithm to count number of leaf nodes in a Binary Tree t and what is its computing time.
129. Explain basic concepts of NP hard and NP Complete problems.
130. Explain the use of asymptotic notations in the analysis of algorithms
131. What type of operations can be performed on string's. Explain at least 2 operations on stringswith algorithms.
132. Write short notes on the following:

    (*i*) Dynamic Programming

    (*ii*) Branch and Bound
133. What do you mean by Time and space complexity? Among Quick Sort, Insertion Sort, Heap Sort, Which algorithm is best to sort the data and why?
134. What are the disadvantages of Binary Search algorithm ? What will be the order of complexity of a Binary Search in the unsuccessful case?
135. Here are 16 integers:

    (*i*) 6 6 79 26 45 75 13 31 62 27 76 33 16 62 47. Sort them using a Quick Sort, Insertion Sort, Heap Sort, Bin Sort, treating them as a pair of digits in a range of 0-9.
136. Let G be a connected and undirected graph. Write an algorithm to find out minimum number of edges to be added to G so that G becomes disconnected. Your algorithm should output such a set of edges. What are time and space requirements of your algorithm?
137. In the following Graph, find out the shortest distance of all the nodes from the node A. Explain with the help of suitable algorithms.
138. What is time and space complexity of "Insertion Sort"? Explain.
139. Write an string processing algorithm to identify whether a particular sequence of character is in string or not.
140. What are the various methods or techniques in which various algorithms can be expressed?
141. What is criterion function in backtracking? What is solution space for backtracking problem? Explain by taking sum of subset as a problem.

142. What is LC Search? How does it help in finding a solution for Branch and Bound Algorithm?

143. Explain algorithm for evaluating a polynomial in coefficient exponent form.

144. What is 8 Queens problem? How does backtracking helps in solving it?

145. What is Greedy Method? Write an algorithm for knapsack problem using Greedy Method.

146. What is Optimal Merge Pattern problem? Merge the files (X_1, X_2 .... X_5)of length 20, 30, 10, 5, 30 respectively. Also represent the merge pattern using Binary Tree.

147. Define Principal of Optimality. Explain 0/1 knapsack problem using Dynamic Programming.

148. What is evaluation and interpolation of Polynomials. Explain by giving a suitable example.

149. Justify the statement "An optimization problem can be solved in the polynomial time if and only if the corresponding decision problem can."

150. Explain the Big Oh notation used in the analysis of algorithm

151. What is the computing time for the following statement:

```
{
for i = 1 to m do
for i = 1 to n do
c[i, j]:= a [i, j] + b [i, j];
}
```

152. Write an algorithm to delete an element from a linked list. Also mention the worst case running time for this operation.

153. Explain the connected and Biconnected components in Graphs.

154. Explain the tree traversal techniques.

155. Using suitable example explain straightforward evaluation of polynomials.

156. Give brief concept of Algebraic Simplification and algebraic transformation.

157. Explain the various path traversal techniques with example.

158. Define Algorithm and also explain the different criterion that all algorithms must satisfy.

159. Explain how to validate and analyze the algorithm.

160. Using the recursive algorithm, explain how the tower of Hanoi problem can be solved. What will be time and space complexity for the algorithms.

161. Algorithm sum (a, n)

```
{
s = 0. 0;
for i = 1 to n do
s = s + a[i];
return s;
} Give computation time
```

162. Explain why we use a asymptotic notation? Also define the following notations Big Oh, Omega, Theta.

163. Explain an algorithm to insert 5 elements in stack and in a Queue.

164. Explain the different terminologies for tree and graph.

165. Explain what do you mean by algebraic problem? Discuss various techniques for algebraic problems.

166. Define Prim's and Kruskal Algorithms.

167. Explain Traveling Salesperson Problem.

168. What do you mean by dynamic programming. Explain All pairs Shortest Path problem with example.

169. Solve 4 Queens Problem using Backtracking.

170. What is dynamic Programming? What is Multi Stage Graph Problem?

171. What do you mean by sorting? What are various sorting Techniques? Explain any two.

172. Solve 0/1 knapsack Problem using Greedy Method.

173. Solve 0/1 knapsack Problem using Dynamic Programming.

174. Explain evaluation and interpolation with example.

175. What is NP Hard and NP Complete? Explain with example.

176. Differentiate between Deterministic and Non-deterministic Algorithms.

177. Explain the algorithm for Quick Sort. On what input does Quick Sort exhibit its worst casebehavior.

178. What is Multi Stage Graph Problem? How does dynamic problem help in solving it?

179. Write short notes on:

(*a*) Approximation Algorithms (*b*) Combinatorial Algorithms

180. Write an algorithm to find *n*th minimum and maximum element using divide and conquer strategy.

181. What is Traveling Salesperson Problem? Find the solution of the following Traveling Salesperson Problem? Find the solution of the following salesman problem.

182. Calculate the number of swaps to sort the following data using bubble sort

$$5, 3, 2, 0, -4, -10, 15, 1$$

183. Give pictorial representation of each pass.

184. What is criterion function and solution space of Backtracking? Explain and solve four Queen's problem using Backtracking.

185. Explain in detail various Set algorithms.

186. What is Greedy method? Give general algorithm for it. State and write Knapsack problem using Greedy Method.

187. Give State space representation for 4 Queen's problem. Number the nodes as in DFS, BFS, D Search.

188. Solve 15 Puzzle Problem using Branch and Bound. Initial arrangement of tiles is given below.

189. By taking suitable example explain how the sum of Subset problem can be solved by using Backtracking algorithm design technique.

190. Explain the following algorithm design techniques; Backtracking, Branch and Bound, Dynamic Programming, and Divide and Conquer.

191. Write and explain the algorithms for Disjoint Set Union if we are given two sets S_i and S_j

192. Define Knapsack problem. Solve the following using Knapsack Problem.

193. $n = 3, m = 20$

194. $(P_1, P_2, P_3) = (24, 25, 15)$

195. $(W_1, W_2, W_3) = (18, 15, 10)$

196. Define Job Sequencing with Deadlines. Solve the following problem using Job.

197. Sequencing with Deadlines:

198. $n = 4, (P_1, P_2, P_3, P_4) = (100, 10, 15, 27)$

199. $(D_1, D_2, D_3, D_4) = (2, 1, 2, 1)$

200. Define Optimal Storage on Tapes. Solve the following using this technique:
$n = 3, (L_1, L_2, L_3) = (5, 10, 3)$.

201. Define Optimal Merge Pattern. Find Optimal Merge pattern for 10 files whose lengths, are 28, 32, 12, 5, 84, 53, 91, 35, 3, 11.

202. Obtain a set of Optimal Huffman Codes for the messages(M_1 .... M_7)with relative frequencies (q_1 .... q_7) = (4, 5, 7, 8, 10, 12, 20). Draw the decode tree for this set of codes.

203. Define the Traveling Salesperson Problem. Solve problem using TSP where the edge lengths are given as:

0	10	15	20
5	0	9	10
6	13	0	12
8	8	9	0

204. What do you mean by deterministic and Non-deterministic Algorithms? Differentiate between them. Write example for each of them.

205. Define NP Hard and NP Complete. Represent the relation between them. Prove that P is a subset of NP.

206. What is Clique Decision Problem. Show that clique optimization reduces to clique decision problem.

207. What are approximation Algorithms? Define absolute approximation and Eapproximation with example.

208. What is Algorithm? Write the various performance analysis techniques of Algorithm Discuss advantages and disadvantages of each.

209. What is data structure? Explain various data structures with examples.

210. Write algorithm for Quick Sort using divide and Conquer .

211. What is Divide and Conquer algorithm. Use this algorithm to find maximum and minimum from a given array.

212. Write an algorithm for Merge Sort using Divide and Conquer.

213. What do you mean by dynamic programming? Explain multistage Graphs using dynamic Programming.

214. What are Strings? What are various String Algorithms? Explain any two of them.

215. Explain 0/1 knapsack problem using any two techniques you know.

216. Explain asymptotic notations. Also explain the following notations:

Big O, Omega, Theta

217. What do you mean by complexity of an algorithm? Define time and space complexity with examples.

218. Explain various traversal techniques for trees.

219. Explain various traversal techniques for graphs.

220. What is Backtracking? Explain various problems solved by backtracking.

221. What is Backtracking? Solve 8 Queens problem by backtracking.

222. Explain various search techniques for trees.

223. Explain various search techniques for graphs.

224. How sum of subset problem is solved by Backtracking.

225. What is graph coloring. Explain it with example. Show that a graph is 4 color able.

226. What do you mean by Branch and Bound? Solve 15-puzzle problem.

227. Define the following:

LC Search

FIFO Branch and Bound

LC branch and Bound.

228. Define Principle of Optimality. Explain how does it holds on the following problems:

knapsack

optimal Merge Pattern

Shortest Path.

SOME SOLVED QUESTIONS

1. What is an Algorithm?

Ans. An algorithm is a sequence of unambiguous instructions for solving a problem, *i.e.*, for obtaining a required output for any legitimate input in a finite amount of time.

2. State the Euclid's algorithm for finding GCD of two given numbers.

Ans. ALGORITHM *Euclid (m, n)*

```
// Computes gcd (m, n) by Euclid's algorithm
//Input: Two nonnegative, not-both-zero integers m and n
//Output: Greatest common divisor of m and n
while n ≠ 0 do
          r ← m mod n
          m ← n
          n ← r
return m.
```

3. What are Sequential Algorithms?

Ans. The central assumption of the RAM model is that instructions are executed one after another, one operation at a time. Accordingly, algorithms designed to be executed on such machines are called Sequential algorithms.

4. What are Parallel Algorithms?

Ans. The central assumption of the RAM model does not hold for some newer computers that can execute operations concurrently, *i.e.*, in parallel algorithms that take advantage of this capability are called Parallel algorithms.

5. What is Exact and Approximation algorithm?

Ans. The principal decision to choose solving the problem exactly is called exact algorithm.

The principal decision to choose solving the problem approximately is called Approximation algorithm.

6. What is Algorithm Design Technique? (*Nov/Dec 2005*)

Ans. An algorithm design technique is a general approach to solving problems algorithmically that is applicable to a variety of problems from different areas of computing.

7. Define Pseudo code.

Ans. A Pseudo code is a mixture of a natural language and programming language like constructs. A pseudo code is usually more precise than a natural language, and its usage often yields more succinct algorithm descriptions.

8. Define Flowchart.

Ans. A method of expressing an algorithm by a collection of connected geometric shapes containing descriptions of the algorithm's steps.

9. Explain Algorithm's Correctness.

Ans. To prove that the algorithm yields a required result for every legitimate input in a finite amount of time. Example: Correctness of Euclid's algorithm for computing the greatest common divisor stems from correctness of the equality gcd (m, n) = gcd $(n, m \bmod n)$.

10. What is Efficiency of algorithm?

Ans. Efficiency of an algorithm can be precisely defined and investigated with mathematical rigor. There are two kinds of algorithm efficiency

(1) Time Efficiency–Indicates how fast the algorithm runs

(2) Space Efficiency–Indicates how much extra memory the algorithm needs.

11. What is generality of an algorithm?

Ans. It is a desirable characteristic of an algorithm. Generality of the problem the algorithm solves is sometimes easier to design an algorithm for a problem posed in more general terms.

12. What is algorithm's Optimality?

Ans. Optimality is about the complexity of the problem that algorithm solves. What is the minimum amount of effort any algorithm will need to exert to solve the problem in question is called algorithm's Optimality.

13. What do you mean by "Sorting" problem?

Ans. The sorting problem asks us to rearrange the items of a given list in ascending order (or descending order).

14. What do you mean by "Searching" problem?

Ans. The searching problem deals with finding a given value, called a search key, in a given set.

15. What do you mean by "Worst case-Efficiency" of an algorithm?

Ans. The "Worst case-Efficiency" of an algorithm is its efficiency for the worst-case input of size n, which is an input (or inputs) of size n for which the algorithm runs the longest among all possible inputs of that size.

Example: If you want to sort a list of numbers in ascending order when the numbers are given in descending order. In this running time will be the longest.

16. What do you mean by "Best case-Efficiency" of an algorithm?

Ans. The "Best case-Efficiency" of an algorithm is its efficiency for the Best-case input of size n, which is an input (or inputs) of size n for which the algorithm runs the fastest among all possible inputs of that size.

Example: If you want to sort a list of numbers in ascending order when the numbers are given in ascending order. In this running time will be the smallest.

17. Define the "Average-case efficiency" of an algorithm?

Ans. The "Average-case efficiency" of an algorithm is its efficiency for the input of size n, for which the algorithm runs between the best case and the worst case among all possible inputs of that size.

18. What do you mean by "Amortized efficiency"?

Ans. The "Amortized efficiency" applies not only a single run of an algorithm but rather to a sequence of operations performed on the same data structure. It turns out that in some situations a single operation can be expensive, but the total time for an entire sequence of n such operations is always significantly better than the worst case efficiency of that single operation multiplied by n. This is known as "Amortized efficiency".

19. How to measure the algorithm's efficiency?

Ans. It is logical to investigate the algorithm's efficiency as a function of some parameter n indicating the algorithm's input size.

Example: It will be the size of the list for problems of sorting, searching, finding the list's smallest element, and most other problems dealing with lists.

20. What is called the basic operation of an algorithm?

Ans. The most important operation of the algorithm is the operation contributing the most to the total running time is called basic operation of an algorithm.

21. How to measure an algorithm's running time?

Ans. Let C_{op} be the time of execution of an algorithm's basic iteration on a particular computer and let C (n) be the number of times this operation needs to be executed for this algorithm. Then we can estimate the running time T(n) of a program implementing this algorithm on that computer by the formula

$$T(n) \approx C_{op}\, C(n)$$

22. Define order of growth.

Ans. The efficiency analysis framework concentrates on the order of growth of an algorithm's basic operation count as the principal indicator of the algorithm's efficiency. To compare and rank such orders of growth we use three notations

(1) O (Big oh) notation

(2) Ω (Big Omega) notation and

(3) Θ (Big Theta) notation

23. Define Big oh notation. *(May/June 2006, April/May 2008)*

Ans. A function $t(n)$ is said to be in O($g(n)$) denoted $t(n)$ ε O ($g(n)$), if $t(n)$ is bounded above by some constant multiple of $g(n)$ for all large n, *i.e.*, if there exist some positive constant c and some non-negative integer n_0 such that

$$T(n) \leq c\, g(n) \text{ for } n \geq n_0$$

24. Prove that $100n + 5 \in O(n^2)$?

Ans. Clearly $100n + 5 \leq 100n + n$ (for all $n \geq 5$) $= 101\, n \leq 101n^2$

By choosing $n_0 = 5$ and $c = 101$ we find that $100n + 5 \in O(n^2)$.

25. Define Ω notation.

Ans. A function $t(n)$ is said to be in Ω ($g(n)$), denoted $t(n) \in \Omega(g(n))$, if $t(n)$ is bounded below by some positive constant multiple of $g(n)$ for all large n, *i.e.*, if there exist some positive constant c and some non-negative integer n_0 such that

$$T(n) \leq c\, g(n) \text{ for } n \geq n_0$$

26. Prove that $n^3 \in \Omega(n^2)$?

Ans. Clearly $n^3 \geq n^2$ for all $n \geq 0$. *i.e.*, we can select $c = 1$ and $n = 0$.

27. Define Θ – notation.

Ans. A function $t(n)$ is said to be in Θ $(g(n))$, denoted $t(n) \in \Theta(g(n))$, if $t(n)$ is bounded both above and below by some positive constant multiples of $g(n)$ for all large n, *i.e.*, if there exist some positive constant c_1 and c_2 and some non negative integer n_0 such that

$$c_2\, g(n) \leq t(n) \leq c_1\, g(n) \text{ for } n \geq n_0$$

28. Prove that(½)n (n – 1) ∈ Θ(n^2).

Ans. $1/2n\,(n-1) = (1/2)n^2 - 1/2n \leq 1/2\,n^2$ for all $n \geq 0$. (we have proved upper inequality) now $1/2n\,(n-1) = (1/2)\,n^2 - 1/2n \geq (1/2)n^2 - 1/2n * 1/2n$ (for all $n \geq 2$) $= 1/4\,n^2$ hence we can select $c_2 = 1/4$, $c_1 = 1/2$ and $n0 = 2$.

29. What is the use of Asymptotic Notations?

Ans. The notations O, Ω and Θ and are used to indicate and compare the asymptotic orders of growth of functions expressing algorithm efficiencies.

30. Explain divide and conquer algorithms.

Ans. Divide and conquer is probably the best known general algorithm design technique. It work according to the following general plan:

(*i*) A problem's instance is divided into several smaller instances of the same problem, ideally of about the same size.

(*ii*) The smaller instances are solved.

(*iii*) If necessary, the solutions obtained for the smaller instances are combined to get a solution to the original problem.

31. Define Merge Sort.

Ans. Merge sort is a perfect example of a successful application of the divide and conquer technique. It sorts a given array A[0...n – l] by dividing it into two halves A[0...[n/2] – 1] and A[[n/2]....n – l], sorting each of them recursively, and then merging the two smaller sorted arrays into a single sorted one.

32. Define Binary Search.

Ans. Binary Search is remarkably efficient algorithm for searching in a sorted array. It works by comparing a search key K with the array's middle element A[m]. If they match, the algorithm stops; Otherwise, the same operation is repeated recursively for the first half of the array if K< A[m] and for the second half if K > A[m]

A[0] ...... A[m – l] A[m] A[m + l] ...... A[n – l]

33. What can we say about the average case efficiency of binary search?

Ans. A sophisticated analysis shows that the average number of key comparisons made by binary search is only slightly smaller than that in the worst case.

$$C_{avg}(n) \approx \log_2 n$$

34. Define Binary Tree.

Ans. A binary tree T is defined as a finite set of nodes that is either empty or consists of s root and two disjoint binary trees T_L, and T_R called, respectively the left and right subtree of the root.

35. How divide and conquer technique can be applied to binary trees?

Ans. Since the binary tree definition itself divides a binary tree into two smaller structures of the same type, the left subtree and the right subtree, many problems about binary trees can be solved by applying the divide-conquer technique.

36. Explain Internal and External Nodes.

Ans. To draw the tree's extension by replacing the empty subtrees by special nodes. The extra nodes shown by little squares are called external. The original nodes shown by little circles are called internal.

37. Define Preorder, inorder and postorder Traversal.

Ans. PREORDER—The root is visited before the left and right subtrees are visited (in that order)

INORDER—The root is visited after visiting its left subtree but before visiting the right Subtree

POSTORDER—The root is visited after visiting the left and right subtrees (in that order)

38. Define the Internal Path Length.

Ans. The Internal Path Length I of an extended binary tree is defined as the sum of the lengths of the paths-taken over all internal nodes-from the root to each internal node.

39. Define the External Path Length.

Ans. The External Path Length E of an extended binary tree is defined as the sum of the lengths of the paths-taken over all external nodes-from the root to each external node.

40. Explain about greedy technique.

Ans. The greedy technique suggests constructing a solution to an optimization problem through a sequence of steps, each expanding a partially constructed solution obtained so far, until a complete solution to the problem is reached. On each step, the choice made must *be feasible, locally optimal and irrevocable.*

41. Define Spanning Tree.

Ans. A Spanning Tree of a connected graph is its connected acyclic subgraph (*i.e.*, a tree) that contains all the vertices of the graph.

42. Define Minimum Spanning Tree.

Ans. A minimum spanning tree of a weighted connected graph is its spanning tree of the smallest weight, where the weight of a tree is defined as the sum of the weights on all its edges.

43. Define min-heap.

Ans. A min-heap is a complete binary tree in which every element is less than or equal to its children. All the principal properties of heaps remain valid for min-heaps, with some obvious modifications.

44. Define Kruskal's Algorithm.

Ans. Kruskal's algorithm looks at a minimum spanning tree for a weighted connected graph G = (V, E) as an acyclic subgraph with | V | – 1 edges for which the sum of the edge weights is the smallest.

45. Define Prim's Algorithm.

Ans. Prim's algorithm is a greedy algorithm for constructing a minimum spanning tree of a weighted connected graph. It works by attaching to a previously constructed subtree a vertex to the vertices already in the tree.

46. Explain Dijkstra's Algorithm.

Ans. Dijkstra's algorithm solves the single-source shortest-path problem of finding shortest paths from a given vertex (the source) to all the other vertices of a weighted graph or digraph. It works as prim's algorithm but compares path lengths rather than edge lengths. Dijkstra's algorithm always yields a correct solution for a graph with nonnegative weights.

47. Define Dynamic Programming.

Ans. Dynamic programming is a technique for solving problems with overlapping problems. Typically, these subproblems arise from a recurrence relating a solution to a given problem with solutions to its smaller subproblems of the same type. Rather than solving overlapping subproblems again and again, dynamic programming suggests solving each of the smaller subproblems only once and recording the results in a table from which we can then obtain a solution to the original problem.

48. Define Binomial Coefficient.

Ans. The Binomial Coefficient, denoted C(n, k) is the number of Combinations (subsets) of k elements from an n-element set($0 < k < n$). The name "binomial coefficients" comes from the participation of these numbers in the so called binomial formula

$$(a + b)^n = (n, 0)a^n + ... + C\,(n, i)a^{n-i}\,b^i + ... + C\,(n, n)b^n$$

49. Define Transitive closure.

Ans. The transitive closure of a directed graph with n vertices can be defined as the n by n Boolean matrix T = {ti,}, in which the element in the ith row ($1 \leq i \leq n$) and the jth column ($l \leq j \leq n$) is 1 if there exists a non trivial directed path from the ith vertex to j^{th} vertex; otherwise , t_{ij} is 0.

50. Explain Warshalls algorithm.

Ans. Warshall's algorithm constructs the transitive closure of a given digraph with n vertices through a series of n by n Boolean matrices $R^{(0)}, ... , R^{(k-l)}\,R^{(k)}, ... , R^{(n)}$

Each of these matrices provides certain information about directed paths in the digraph.

51. Explain All-pair shortest-paths problem.

Ans. Given a weighted connected graph (undirected or directed), the all pairs shortest paths problem asks to find the distances (the lengths of the shortest path) from each vertex to all other vertices.

52. Explain Floyd's algorithm.

Ans. It is convenient to record the lengths of shortest paths in an n by n matrix D called the distance matrix: the element d_{ij} in the ith row and the jth column of this matrix indicates the length of the shortest path from the ith vertex to the jth vertex. We can generate the distance matrix with an algorithm that is very similar to warshall's algorithm. It is called Floyd's algorithm.

53. What does Floyd's algorithm do?

Ans. It is used to find the distances (the lengths of the shortest paths) from each vertex to all other vertices of a weighted connected graph.

54. Explain principle of Optimality.

Ans. It says that an optimal solution to any instance of an optimization problem is composed of optimal solutions to its subinstances.

55. Explain Optimal Binary Search Trees.

Ans. One of the principal application of Binary Search Tree is to implement the operation of searching. If probabilities of searching for elements of a set are known, it is natural to pose a question about an optimal binary search tree for which the average number of comparisons in a search is the smallest possible.

56. Explain Knapsack problem.

Ans. Given n items of known weights $w_1, w_2 ...... w_n$ and values $v_1, v_2 ...... v_n$ and a knapsack of capacity W, find the most valuable subset of the items that fit into the knapsack. (Assuming all the weights and the knapsack's capacity are positive integers the item values do not have to be integers).

57. Explain the Memory Function technique.

Ans. The Memory Function technique seeks to combine strengths of the top down and bottom-up approaches to solving problems with overlapping subproblems. It does this by solving, in the top-down fashion but only once, just necessary subproblems of a given problem and recording their solutions in a table.

58. Explain "Traveling salesman problem".

Ans. A salesman has to travel n cities starting from any one of the cities and visit the remaining cities exactly once and come back to the city where he started his journey in such a manner that either the distance is minimum or cost is minimum. This is known as traveling salesman problem.

59. Explain Backtracking.

Ans. The principal idea is to construct solutions one component at a time and evaluate such partially constructed candidates as follows.

- If a partially constructed solution can be developed further without violating the problem's constraints, it is done by taking the first remaininig legitimate option for the next component.
- If there is no legitimate option for the next component, no alternatives for any remaining component need to be considered.

In this case, the algorithm backtracks to replace the last component of the partially constructed solution with its next option.

60. Explain State Space Tree.

Ans. If it is convenient to implement backtracking by constructing a tree of choices being made, the tree is called a state space tree. Its root represents an initial state before the search for a solution begins.

61. Explain promising and non-promising node.

Ans. A node in a state space tree is said to be promising if it corresponds to a partially constructed solution that may still lead to a complete solution, otherwise it is called non-promising

62. Explain *n*-Queens problem.

Ans. The problem is to place n queens on an n by n chessboard so that no two queens attack each other by being in the same row or same column or on the same diagonal.

63. Explain Subset-Sum Problem.

Ans. We consider the subset-sum problem: Find a subset of a given

set $S = \{S_1, S_2, \ldots\ldots S_n\}$ of n positive integers whose sum is equal to a given positive integer d.

64. Explain Branch and Bound Technique.

Ans. Compared to backtracking, branch and bound requires

The idea to be strengthened further if we deal with an optimization problem, one that seeks to minimize or maximize an objective function, usually subject to some constraints.

65. Define Feasible Solution.

Ans. A feasible solution is a point in the problem's search space that satisfies all the problem's constraints.

Example: A Hamiltonian Circuit in the traveling salesman problem. A subset of items whose total weight does not exceed the knapsack's Capacity.

66. Define Optimal solution.

Ans. Is a feasible solution with the best value of the objective function.

Example: The shortest Hamiltonian Circuit.

The most valuable subset of items that fit the knapsack.

67. Mention two reasons to terminate a search path at the current node in a state-space tree of a branch and bound algorithm.

Ans. The value of the node's bound is not better than the value of the best solution seen so far. The node represents no feasible solutions because the constraints of the problem are already violated.

68. Explain "Graph coloring" problem.

Ans. The graph coloring problem asks us to assign the smallest number of colors to vertices of a graph so that no two adjacent vertices are the same color.

69. Explain Knapsack Problem.

Ans. Find the most valuable subset of n items of given positive integer weights and values that fit into a knapsack of a given positive integer capacity.

70. Define tractable and intractable problems.

Ans. Problems that can be solved in polynomial time are called tractable problems, problems that cannot be solved in polynomial time are called intractable problems.

71. Explain the theory of computational complexity.

Ans. A problem's intractability remains the same for all principal models of computations and all reasonable input encoding schemes for the problem under consideration.

72. Explain class P problems.

Ans. Class P is a class of decision problems that can be solved in polynomial time by (deterministic) algorithms. This class of problems is called polynomial.

73. Explain undecidable problems.

Ans. If the decision problem cannot be solved in polynomial time, and if the decision problems cannot be solved at all by any algorithm. Such problems are called Undecidable.

74. Explain the halting problem.

Ans. Given a computer program and an input to it, determine whether the program will halt on that input or continue working indefinitely on it.

75. Explain class NP problems.

Ans. Class NP is the class of decision problems that can be solved by nondeterministic polynomial algorithms. Most decision problems are in NP. First of all, this class includes all the problems in P. This class of problems is called Nondeterministic polynomial.

76. Explain NP-complete problems.

Ans. A decision problem d is said to be NP-complete if

(*i*) it belongs to class NP

(*ii*) every problem in NP is polynomially reducible to D.

77. When a decision problem is said to be polynomially reducible?

Ans. A decision problem D_1 is said to be polynomially reducible to a decision problem D_2 if there exists a function t that transforms instances of D_1 to instances of D_2 such that

(*i*) t maps all yes instances of d_1 to yes instances odf d_2 and all no instances of d_1 to no instances of d_2

(*ii*) t is computable by a polynomial time algorithm.

78. Define a Heuristic.

Ans. A heuristic is a common-sense rule drawn from experience rather than from a mathematically proved assertion.

Example: Going to the nearest unvisited city in the traveling salesman problem is a good illustration for Heuristic.

79. Explain NP-Hard problems.

Ans. The notion of an NP-hard problem can be defined more formally by extending the notion of polynomial reducability to problems that are not necessary in class NP including optimization problems.

80. Define Traversals.

Ans. When the search necessarily involves the examination of every vertex in the object being searched it is called a traversal.

81. List out the techniques for traversals in graph.

Ans. Breadth first search

Depth first search

82. What is articulation point?

Ans. A vertex v in a connected graph G is an articulation point if and only if the deletion of vertex v together with all edged incident to v disconnects the graph in to two or more nonempty components.

VIVA QUESTIONS

Q.1. What are the factors which affects the running time of an algorithm?

Q.2. Which is asymptotically larger log(log*n) or log*(log n) ?

Q.3. Solve using Merge sort following sequence

25, 19, 18, 6, 15, 10, 1, 5, 7, 13

Q.4. What are the elements of dynamic programming?

Q.5. What is feasible and optimal solution in greedy method?

Q.6. What is the potential method in case of amortized analysis?

Q.7. What is backtracking method?

Q.8. What is branch and bound method?

Q.9. What is the running time of DFS and BFS?

Q.10. What is the difference between deterministic and non-deterministic problems?

Q.11. What is NP hard and NP completeness?

Q.12. What is subset and ordering paradigm?

Q.13. What is optimization problem?

Q.14. Give the examples of subset paradigm?

Q.15. What is best, average and worst case?

NUMERICAL PROBLEM

1. Write an algorithm for tower of Hanoi problem?
2. Suppose we have n totals elements divided into m sorted lists. How to produce a single sorted list of all n elements in time O($n$log n)?
3. Solve the following recurrence relation:

   (*i*) $T(n) = 3T(n/2) + n\log n$

   (*ii*) $T(n) = 7T(n/2) + n^2$

   (*iii*) $T(n) = T(n/2) + c$.
4. Create a max heap and min heap

   20, 10, 5, 4, 25, 70, 60, 40.
5. Show that quick sort running time in average case is O($n$log n).

6. Sort the following list using quick sort

   3, 1, 4, 2, 5, 9, 7, 6, 8, 9, 0.

7. Show that the following matrices would be multiplied using Strassen's algorithm.

$$A = \begin{bmatrix} 7 & 9 \\ 2 & 5 \end{bmatrix} \quad B = \begin{bmatrix} 3 & 2 \\ 6 & 5 \end{bmatrix}$$

8. Create a B-tree of the following list:

   L = {K, J, G, F, C, B, A, D, E, H, I, L, M}

   Given minimization factor $t = 3$, minimum degree = 2, and maximum degree = 5.

9. Solve the 0/1 knapsack problem

   $n = 3$, $(w_1, w_2, w_3) = (2, 3, 3)$, $(p_1, p_2, p_3) = (1, 2, 4)$ and $m = 6$ find optimal solution.

10. Find the optimal merge pattern for following data

    28, 32, 12, 5, 84, 53, 91, 35, 3, 11.

11. Consider the knapsack instance $n = 3$, $(w_1, w_2, w_3) = (2, 3, 4)$ and $(p_1, p_2, p_3) = (1, 2, 5)$, $m = 5$. Find the optimal solution.

12. Evaluate subset sum for the following set:

    S = {3, 4, 5, 6}

    X = 9

13. Solve the 4 queens problem using backtracking.

14. Solve the TSP problem having the following cost matrix using branch and bound techniques.

$$\begin{array}{c} \\ A \\ B \\ C \\ D \end{array} \begin{array}{c} \begin{array}{cccc} A & B & C & D \end{array} \\ \begin{bmatrix} x & 5 & 2 & 3 \\ 4 & x & 2 & 3 \\ 4 & 2 & x & 3 \\ 7 & 6 & 8 & x \end{bmatrix} \end{array}$$

15. Find the DFS and BFS of the given graph

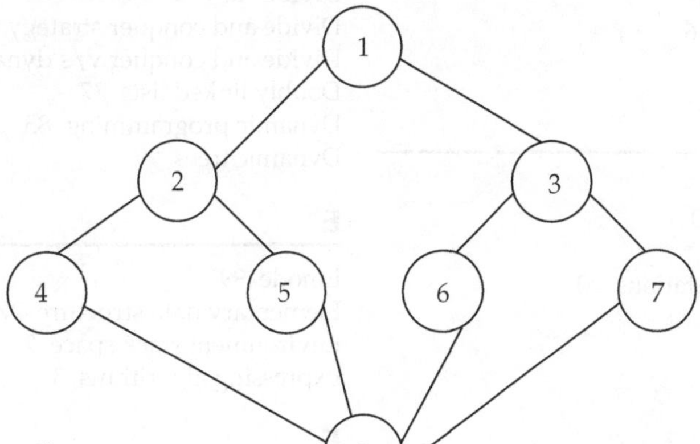

INDEX

A

B

C

D

E

F

R

S

T

V

W